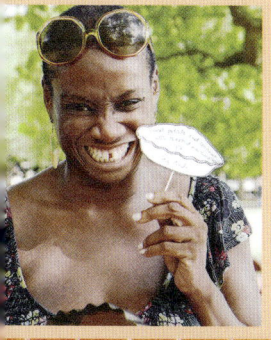

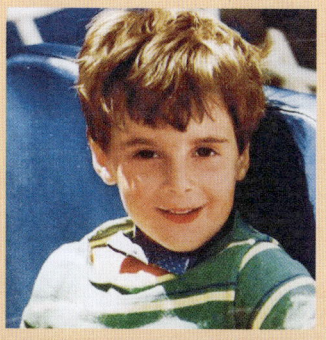

# LEON

## HAPPY BAKING

BY CLAIRE PTAK & HENRY DIMBLEBY

# LEON

# HAPPY BAKING

BY CLAIRE PTAK & HENRY DIMBLEBY

conran
OCTOPUS

# CONTENTS

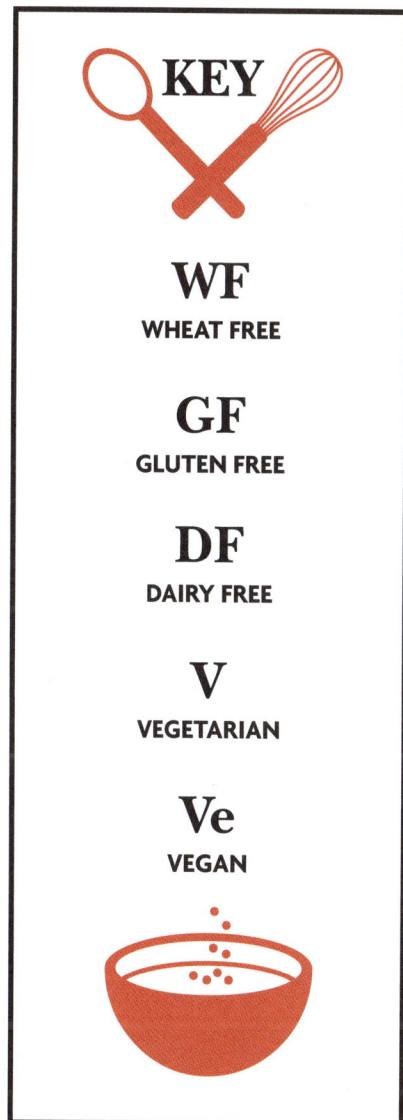

# WELCOME TO LEON HAPPY BAKING

*Leon was founded on the belief that food should both taste good and do you good. In this book we hope to show that this can be the case even where it is often thought impossible – when cooking comfort food. The dishes you will find here look indulgent, sound naughty and taste like the sort of treats that normally come with a side-helping of guilt. Yet many of the recipes are wheat, dairy or refined sugar free, with plenty of vegan and gluten-free options.*

*We want this book to be accessible to even the most inexperienced cook – hence our Baking Basics section at the back on ingredients and techniques. Once you have mastered a recipe you can use our suggested variations to put your own stamp on it. We also want to provide inspiration for the more experienced. Some of the recipes are daring (see Baked Alaska page 182), some draw on ancient wisdom (see Sourdough Bread page 21) and some are downright show stopping (see Leon's Birthday Cake page 126) – but even the more adventurous recipes shouldn't prove too tricky for the careful amateur.*

*We hope this book finds a permanent place in your kitchen and becomes batter-smattered, tacky with toffee and dog-eared through use.*

*Henry & Claire*

**KEY**

**WF**
WHEAT FREE

**GF**
GLUTEN FREE

**DF**
DAIRY FREE

**V**
VEGETARIAN

**Ve**
VEGAN

# BREADS

# BREAD – THE BASICS

## TYPES OF BREAD

All breads fall into four main categories, defined by what makes them rise:

### SOURDOUGH

Sourdough is the most ancient form of leavened bread. It is made with a sourdough starter (see page 18), which can either be taken from someone else's existing starter or created by leaving wheat and water to ferment naturally. The starter contains a symbiotic combination of natural yeasts and lactobacillus culture. It is the culture that creates the lactic acid that gives this bread its distinctive sour taste.

Sourdough has a reputation for being frustrating and unpredictable if you don't make it all the time, because the starter needs attention. But starters are surprisingly robust – Henry, being chaotic and absent-minded, has had to bring many a forgotten and slimy starter back to life.

The thing that takes a bit of getting used to is the timing – the cycle for making a loaf is a minimum of twelve hours, and typically twenty-four. But the actual work involved is minimal (most of that time is spent waiting for the dough to rise), and the reward is a uniquely flavoured loaf that stays fresh for over a week.

### YEASTED BREADS

Most bread is risen using baker's yeast, *Saccharomyces cerevisiae*. It is the same yeast that is used to brew alcohol. It feeds on the sugars in the wheat and converts them into carbon dioxide, the gas that causes the bread to rise. It is easier to use than a sourdough starter because it does not require looking after and it is a good deal more vigorous – a loaf can rise in a couple of hours in a warm room. You can buy yeast fresh in blocks or dried in granules.

If you have not made bread before, this is where to start. The spelt loaf on page 14 is outrageously easy to make and equally impressive. You can also experiment with different flour mixtures and flavourings to create your own signature loaf.

If you have some sourdough starter in the fridge, you can add a little to traditionally yeasted breads to get a touch of the flavour in under half the time.

### SODA BREAD

This bread uses bicarbonate of soda as its raising agent. Wheat flour is mixed with buttermilk (or sometimes yoghurt) and the lactic acid reacts with the soda to create bubbles of carbon dioxide, which raise the bread.

It is a relatively modern bread, having become popular in Ireland in the mid-nineteenth century as a cheaper and faster alternative to yeast. It has a wonderful soft, cakey texture and a distinctive taste.

### UNLEAVENED BREAD

This is a dough that requires no raising agent at all. It is the easiest of all breads to make.

# FLOUR STATION RYE BREAD

**MAKES: 1 LARGE LOAF**
**PREP TIME: 1 HOUR + COOLING AND RISING · COOK TIME: 55 MINS–1 HOUR**
**WF · V (DF · Ve** if oil is used for greasing)

25g **rye flour starter** (50:50 rye flour and water; see Sourdough Starter on page 18)

**butter** or **oil**, for greasing

500g **rye flour,** plus extra for dusting

1 medium **potato**

250ml lukewarm **water**

2 tablespoons **molasses**

100g **sunflower seeds**

1½ x 7g sachets **dried active yeast**

2 teaspoons **fine sea salt**

*This bread, which we use at Leon to make open sandwiches, is baked for us by the magnificent bakers at London's Flour Station.*

First, make your starter according to the recipe on page 18, using rye flour.

Heat the oven to 200°C/400°F/gas mark 6. Grease a 900g/2lb loaf tin and dust it with rye flour.

Prick the skin of the potato and bake it in the oven for 1 hour. Let cool, then scoop the flesh into a mixing bowl and mash until smooth. You need 150g of potato.

Add the remaining ingredients to the bowl with the mashed potato, ensuring the yeast and salt don't make contact. Fit the bowl into a free-standing mixer fitted with a dough hook and mix on a slow speed until all is well combined and a soft, sticky dough has formed. You can do this by hand, too – just use a lot of elbow-grease.

Tip the dough onto a lightly floured surface, shape into a loaf and place in the prepared tin. Dust the top of the loaf with more rye flour, then cover the tin with a damp tea towel and leave to rise in a warm place for about 12 hours (overnight is easiest), until the dough has almost doubled in size. Heat the oven to 220°C/425°F/ gas mark 7 and place a baking tray in the bottom of the oven to heat up. Fill a jug with 200ml of water and have it ready.

Dust the loaf with rye flour again and place on the middle shelf of the oven. Quickly pour the water into the baking tray, then immediately close the oven door – this will create steam, which helps the bread develop a good crust. Bake for 55 minutes– 1 hour, until the loaf has a rich dark crust and sounds hollow when tapped on the bottom. Turn out and cool on a wire rack.

## ≡ TIP ≡

This bread actually improves with age and is best enjoyed the day after baking. It will stay fresh for at least a week, as the potatoes attract moisture and therefore keep the bread moist for longer.

# SPELT BREAD

MAKES: 3 LOAVES

PREP TIME: 10 MINS + RISING · COOK TIME: 40 MINS

V (**DF** · **Ve** if oil is used for greasing)

**butter** or **oil**, for greasing

1.5kg **strong wholemeal spelt flour**

2 x 7g sachets of **dried quick yeast**

2 tablespoons **sea salt**, crushed

125g **pine nuts**

125g **pumpkin seeds**

125g **sunflower seeds**

125ml **extra virgin olive oil**

900ml–1 litre warm **water**

50g **sunflower seeds** and **nuts**, to sprinkle

## ═ TIPS ═

These freeze really well in freezer bags, but don't keep bread in the fridge as it goes stale more quickly.

You can use normal wholemeal flour if you can't get hold of spelt. Or if you like your loaf lighter you can replace 500g of the wholemeal with strong white flour.

Experiment with various additions. Breads with nuts and fruit can be amazing. Try date and almond, or apricot and walnut.

Add herbs and spices: rosemary, dill and oregano are all interesting.

*This is a bread that Henry has been baking for years, at his wife's insistence. It is very easy to make and impossible to get wrong. It is also a great recipe to play with – adding nuts and seeds, mixing in spices, and using different flours.*

Grease 3 x 900g/2lb loaf tins.

Mix all the dry ingredients (except the seeds for the top) together in a bowl large enough to knead the dough in.

Add the oil, then the water, stirring until the mixture sticks together. Knead in the bowl for a few minutes, until smooth. You can add a little flour if it is too sticky, but remember the maxim – wetter is better. It doesn't matter if a little of the dough sticks to your hands.

Cut into 3 pieces, shape into vague ovals, then put into the loaf tins. Cut a pattern of deep gashes on the top and sprinkle the seeds and nuts into the gashes, then sprinkle a little spelt flour (or bran if you have some to hand) all over.

Put the tins into a large plastic bin bag and tuck the ends of the bag under the tins, leaving them enclosed with plenty of air. Leave until the dough has doubled in size. This will take about 2 hours in a warm kitchen.

Heat the oven to 230°C/450°F/gas mark 8. Bake the loaves for 20 minutes, then turn down the temperature to 200°C/400°F/gas mark 6 for a further 20 minutes. Turn out and cool on a rack.

# RAAB THE BAKER'S CRUSTY WHITE ROLLS

MAKES: 10–12
PREP TIME: 30 MINS + RISING · COOK TIME: 20 MINS
V

150–200ml warm **water**

20g **fresh yeast**

100ml warm **milk**

a pinch of **sugar**

450g **strong white flour**

1 teaspoon **salt**

50g **white vegetable shortening**, cut into cubes, or **vegetable oil**, plus extra for greasing

handful of **ice cubes**

*These crispy rolls are inspired by a family baker in Islington, London.*

Put the water into a bowl, add the yeast, and stir to dissolve. Add the milk and a pinch of sugar to help activate the yeast.

Place the flour, salt and shortening on a work surface, making a well in the middle (if using vegetable oil, add it in the next step).

Pour the liquid yeast mixture (and oil, if using) into the well and gradually blend it into the flour using your hands to form a dough. Add a little more flour to prevent sticking and knead for 10–12 minutes, until a smooth elastic dough is achieved.

Place the dough in a greased bowl, cover it with a damp tea towel, and leave it to rest in a warm place for an hour, or until it has doubled in size.

Tip the dough on to a floured work surface and divide it into 10–12 pieces, about 50g each. Shape them into rounds, pressing down with your hands in a circular motion.

Place the rolls on a lined or well-greased baking tray, leaving enough room for the rolls not to touch once they have risen. Cut a slit in the top of each roll with a sharp knife. Cover with a tea towel.

Preheat the oven to 220°C/425°F/gas mark 7 and place an empty baking tray at the bottom of the oven. When the rolls have doubled in size, remove the tea towel and place the tray in the oven. Throw the ice cubes on to the hot empty baking tray at the bottom of the oven (see tip). Bake the rolls for 15–20 minutes, until golden brown.

## ═ TIP ═

The ice cubes create steam, which is essential for a crusty roll.

# SOURDOUGH STARTER

. . . . . . . . . . . . . . . . . . . . . . . . . . . . . . . . . . . . . . . . . . . . . . . . . . . . . . . . . . . . . . .

**DF · V · Ve** (**WF** if you use rye flour)

. . . . . . . . . . . . . . . . . . . . . . . . . . . . . . . . . . . . . . . . . . . . . . . . . . . . . . . . . . . . . . .

*If you can't find a kindly soul to give you some starter, here are tips on how to make one – courtesy of master baker Tom Herbert, of Hobbs House Bakery in Gloucestershire, who gave Henry a piece of the starter that has been handed down in his family for 55 years.*

. . . . . . . . . . . . . . . . . . . . . . . . . . . . . . . . . . . . . . . . . . . . . . . . . . . . . . . . . . . . . . .

**STARTING A SOURDOUGH**

Find a suitable container to house your sourdough – a kilner jar is ideal. Clean it well and weigh it while empty, noting the weight on an address tag or label (this will save you having to empty it out to know how much you have left in the future).

Weigh 100g of organic wholemeal, dark rye or wholemeal spelt flour (these all work really well) and 100g of warm water into your jar and stir. Leave the jar in a prominent and warm place in your kitchen (this will be its second home), with the lid sealed.

Each day for a week repeat the feeding process. Put 100g of the starter in a bowl (take out the surplus and use to flavour cakes, buns, pancakes and pizza dough), add 100g of water and 100g of flour and stir vigorously to remove all floury lumps with a clean finger or a fork. Return it to the empty jar.

After about 5 days you'll notice bubbles in the dough – like the first windy smile of a baby. You can start to use it after a week, but it'll be slow, weak and infantile. From now on, you can keep it in the fridge (its first home), removing it a couple of days before use to feed it back into full bubbly liveliness

(using 100g of starter, 100g of flour and 100g of water as before). After a month, the dough will have matured and you'll get a better, more even flavour and rising performance.

If it is not performing well enough, try taking it out of the fridge and giving it an extra feed. Remember that it is a living culture – if it's not hibernating in the fridge where it can survive for several months – and it likes to be fed, kept warm and aerated (stirred/whisked). If it dies you'll know because it'll smell like a dead dog on a hot day. Bin the lot and start again.

I'm the custodian of our family sourdough, which has been raising award-winning loaves at Hobbs House Bakery for more than 55 years. Who will you leave your sourdough to in your will?

Peace and loaf,

Tom Herbert

# SOURDOUGH BREAD

MAKES: 1 LOAF

PREP TIME: 45 MINS + RISING · COOK TIME: 35–40 MINS

DF · V · Ve

**SPONGE:**

180ml **water** at about 27°C/80°F

100g **sourdough starter** (see page 18); brought to room temperature

340g **strong white flour** (see tip)

½ teaspoon **fine sea salt**

**DOUGH:**

90ml **water** at about 27°C/80°F

400g **strong white flour**

1 tablespoon **fine sea salt**

*There are two stages to making a sourdough: the 'sponge' – a reinvigorated starter – and the 'dough'.*

The sponge: In a medium bowl or container which will fit into your fridge, combine the water, starter and strong white flour with a wooden spoon.

It is fine if there are lumps of flour or starter because as the sponge starts working it will all meld together. It will have a wonderfully soft and bouncy consistency – too wet to form a dough at this stage.

Set this aside in a warm area of your kitchen, draped with a clean cloth or clingfilm. Ideally the temperature should be in the upper 20's°C. This is easy on a hot summer's day, but in the winter or spring, you might put it near the radiator or the oven while doing other cooking. Let the sponge rise for 4 hours.

The dough: Put the sponge into a mixing bowl. You can mix by hand, of course, but if you have a free-standing mixer with a dough hook, it will make the job easier. Add all of the dough ingredients and mix for about 8–10 minutes. You should end up with a smooth and elastic dough that is just slightly tacky.

If you must knead by hand to feel like you are really making bread, then now is your chance. You really don't need to put flour down on your work surface, so avoid this temptation. Once smooth and elastic, put the dough back in the bowl, cover it again and place it back in its warm spot for 3–4 hours.

RECIPE CONTINUES →

Line a bowl with a muslin cloth or a clean tea towel and generously dust it with flour. Turn the dough out on to your work surface and bash it around a bit to knock some of the air out. This also gets the yeasts acting again. Then shape it into a round loaf shape. Plop the dough into the flour-lined bowl and cover it with another cloth. Let it sit in the warm spot for about 5 hours.

This is very important: turn your oven on a good 45 minutes before you are ready to bake. Get it good and hot, as hot as your oven will go. Claire uses an oven thermometer to check that it is at its maximum before proceeding.

Put a baking tray into the oven to get it really hot, and place another baking tray, with a rimmed edge (to hold a shallow depth of water) on the floor of your oven. Prepare a jug of water next to the oven, ready to pour into the tray. Now, uncover your loaf.

When everything is ready, remove the hot baking tray from the oven and quickly close the door. It is so important to keep the heat in there. Now, turn the dough out onto the baking tray and slice four slits into the top in the shape of a square (or you can develop your own signature cut).

Quickly open the oven, slide the baking tray in, and pour a few glugs of water into the tray on the floor of your oven (be careful the steam does not burn your hand) and slam the door fast.

Set your timer for 20 minutes, and don't peek until the timer has gone off. Then take a look – the loaf should be golden and sound hollow when tapped. You may find it will need 15–20 minutes more. Claire likes her loaf to get nice and dark, even burnt in places. Cool on a wire rack.

≡ TIP ≡

Organic flour makes a big difference here. The chemicals used to kill pests on the growing wheat will also kill the good organisms needed for the bread to rise properly when using a natural yeast.

# GLUTEN-FREE BREAD

MAKES: 1 LOAF

PREP TIME: 20 MINS + RISING · COOK TIME: 55 MINS

WF · GF · V

500g **gluten-free brown bread flour**

½ teaspoon **sea salt**

2 x 7g sachets of **gluten-free dried quick yeast**

2 tablespoons **honey**

325ml **milk**

1 tablespoon **cider vinegar**

2 tablespoons **olive oil**

2 **free-range eggs**

**poppy seeds**, to sprinkle

*The gluten in a loaf gives it that chewy interior and tender crumb. Take the gluten out and you get something a little denser of crumb and a bit more cake-like. In its own right, however, it is very satisfying.*

Grease a 450g/1lb loaf tin.

Combine the flour, salt and yeast in a large bowl and set aside.

Warm the honey and milk slightly and remove from the heat. Add the vinegar and oil and whisk in the eggs.

Add the wet ingredients to the dry ingredients and bring together to form a dough. Then shape the dough into a log. Place it in your prepared tin, sprinkle with water and then scatter poppy seeds over the top, to cover. Put the dough in a warm place and leave to rise for 1 hour.

Heat the oven to 200°C/400°F/gas mark 6 and bake for 45–55 minutes.

Leave the loaf to cool in the tin for 5 minutes before turning out on to a wire rack to cool completely.

## ≡ TIP ≡

Try adding some seeds to the dough to vary the texture and flavour of this loaf. It is always a good idea to soak the seeds overnight before adding them to the bread mixture, because soaking the seeds increases the amount of vitamins your body can absorb from them.

# BALLYMALOE BROWN SODA BREAD

MAKES: 1 LARGE LOAF OR 2 SMALL LOAVES
PREP TIME: 10 MINS · COOK TIME: 40 MINS
V

300g **brown wholemeal flour** (preferably stone-ground)

300g **plain flour**

2 teaspoons **sea salt**

2 teaspoons **bicarbonate of soda**, sieved

550ml **buttermilk** or **sour milk**

*A classic version of this yeast-free, cakey, breakfast bread, created for* **Ballymaloe Cookery Course** *by Darina Allen (Kyle, 2001).*

Heat the oven to 230°C/450°F/gas mark 8.

Mix all the dry ingredients together in a large wide bowl, then make a well in the centre and pour in all the buttermilk or sour milk.

Using one hand, stir in a full circle, starting in the centre and working towards the outside of the bowl until all the flour is incorporated. The dough should be soft but not too wet and sticky. When it all comes together, in a matter of seconds, turn it out on to a well-floured board.

Wash and dry your hands.

Roll the dough around gently with floury hands for a second, just enough to tidy it up. Flip it over and flatten slightly, to about 5cm.

Sprinkle a little flour on to a baking tray and place the loaf on top of the flour.

Make a deep cross with a knife on top of the loaf and bake in the oven for 15–20 minutes. Reduce the heat to 200°C/400°F/gas mark 6 and bake for approximately 15–20 minutes more, or until the bread sounds hollow when tapped (in some ovens it may be necessary to turn the bread over for 5–10 minutes before the end of baking to cook the other side).

Cool on a wire rack.

## ≡ TIP ≡

You can add 12g of fine oatmeal, 1 egg and 12g of softened butter to the above to make a richer soda bread dough.

# FLATBREAD WITH ZA'ATAR

MAKES: 10

PREP TIME: 30 MINS + RISING · COOK TIME: 10 MINS

DF · V · Ve

1 x 7g sachet **dried quick yeast**

100ml warm **water**

3 tablespoons **olive oil**

280g **fine semolina**

70g **'00' flour**

1 teaspoon **sea salt**

10 teaspoons **za'atar**

*This flatbread actually contains a small amount of yeast, which gives it a little lift. The texture of the dough is very dry while you are making it and feels similar to a pasta dough. Both fine semolina and '00' flour are available in many supermarkets and small delis. They are worth seeking out for their unique texture.*

Dissolve the yeast in the warm water in the bottom of a large mixing bowl. Pour in the olive oil, add the semolina, flour and salt, and mix it all together roughly with your hands or a wooden spoon to make a dough.

Cover the bowl and set the dough in a warm place to rise for about 1½ hours.

When the dough has rested, divide it into 10 pieces and roll each piece into a ball. Cover with a clean cloth and let the dough rest again for 10 minutes.

Heat the oven to 230°C/450°F/gas mark 8.

Flatten each ball of dough with your hands (roughly 1–2mm thick) and cover with a damp towel for about 30 minutes.

Sprinkle the flatbreads with za'atar and place on baking trays in the oven for about 10 minutes, until crisp and golden. Cool on a wire rack.

## ═ TIPS ═

Za'atar is a flavouring which can be found in larger supermarkets, Middle Eastern shops or delis. If you can't find it you can make your own, by grinding together dried thyme, sesame seeds and sumac. Cumin, coriander and nigella seeds also work well.

You could also make the flatbreads without za'atar – sprinkle with a little flaky sea salt once cooked and serve with really good green olive oil.

# SAVOURY BAKES

# PIZZA DOUGH

MAKES: 2 PIZZAS

PREP TIME: 30 MINS + RISING · COOK TIME: 15 MINS

DF · V · Ve

1 teaspoon **dried quick yeast**

300–350ml **water**

500g **'00' flour,** plus extra for dusting

**olive oil**

*This is a softer, thicker version of pizza dough than the thin-crust pizzas that are everywhere at the moment. It is super-easy to make and super-comforting to eat.*

In a large bowl, dissolve the yeast in 100ml of the water. You can use water slightly warm from the tap for this, but use cold water for the rest of the dough.

Once the yeast has dissolved, add the flour and then up to 200ml more water. Mix well to form a soft, pliable dough. Cover and allow it to rest for 10 minutes, then decide at that point whether or not to add the remaining 50ml of cold water.

Knead the dough in the bowl until it is smooth and soft. If you like, you can add about 100g of sourdough starter (see page 18) to the dough at this point to give it a lovely sour flavour. Rub a little oil on the dough and cover the bowl with a cloth for 30 minutes.

Once the dough has rested you need to add air by kneading it for 5 minutes every 30 minutes. Do this three times.

Now leave the dough to rise without touching it for 90 minutes in a warmish place in your kitchen.

Heat the oven to 200°C/400°F/gas mark 6. Dust 2 baking trays with flour or line them with baking paper. Divide the dough into 2 pieces and gently press each piece out into a rectangular shape. Don't roll the dough or you will squeeze the air out of it. Irregularity in the dough is what you are striving for.

Drizzle the dough with olive oil and cover it with the topping of your choice. Bake for about 15 minutes, or until golden.

## ═ SUGGESTED TOPPINGS ═

Our favourite topping at the moment is potato & rosemary (pictured overleaf, left). You will need olive oil, 2 baking potatoes (peeled and sliced 2mm thick), 200g mascarpone cheese, 200ml double cream, a sprig of fresh rosemary and salt and pepper to taste. Rub the dough with oil, arrange the potato slices on top, dot with the cheese and pour over the cream. Scatter rosemary leaves over the top and season with salt and pepper.

Other toppings we like:
• Prosciutto, crème fraîche, sage
• Halved cherry tomatoes, salami, mozzarella, finely chopped dried chilli
• Sausagemeat, fennel seeds, crème fraîche, blanched broccoli (pictured overleaf, right)
• Stilton, walnut, endive or other chicory

# OATMEAL BISCUITS

MAKES: 12
PREP TIME: 15 MINS + CHILLING · COOK TIME: 12–15 MINS
V

250g **oatmeal**, stone-ground or fine
150g **spelt flour**, plus extra for dusting
100g **wholemeal spelt flour**
½ teaspoon **bicarbonate of soda**
250g **unsalted butter**
1 teaspoon **salt**
1 **free-range egg**

*These biscuits are buttery and crumbly and the best thing to eat with a hard British cheese. A Christmas essential with Stilton.*

Mix together the oatmeal, spelt flours and bicarbonate of soda. Rub the butter into the oatmeal mix between your fingertips until it just about disappears.

Add the salt and egg to bring the dough together, then chill for at least 30 minutes.

Meanwhile heat the oven to 180°C/350°F/gas mark 4 and line a baking tray with baking paper.

Roll out the dough to about 3mm thickness on a lightly floured surface. Cut out the biscuits with a round cutter. Alternatively, cut a circle of dough 18cm in diameter and then cut that into 4 wedges, to make 4 large biscuits.

Place the biscuits on the baking tray and cook in the oven for 12–15 minutes. They will crisp up as they cool. They can be eaten fresh or kept in a tin for up to a week.

## ═ TIP ═

These biscuits will absorb moisture and become soft if left out, but they can be re-crisped (as can any biscuits containing butter) by laying them out on a baking tray lined with baking paper and popping them into a preheated oven at 160°C/325°F/gas mark 3 for 5 minutes.

# HENRY'S SPICED CHICKEN MYSTERY PIE

**SERVES: 4–6**

**PREP TIME: 10 MINS + COOLING · COOK TIME: 2¾ HOURS**

1 large **chicken**

**olive oil**, for rubbing

300g **rhubarb**, cut into 2.5cm pieces

2 **bay leaves**

4 **cardamom pods**, crushed with the
   back of a knife

1 glass of **white wine**

2 **onions**, peeled and sliced vertically
   into 8 wedges

1 tablespoon **turmeric**

150ml **double cream**

1 x 350g packet of ready-made **puff pastry**
   (or **flaky pastry** from page 212)

1 **free-range egg**, to glaze

**salt** and freshly ground **black pepper**

*The mystery is that no one can believe it's made with rhubarb. The pink stems are wonderful in savoury dishes, adding body and a subtle citrus flavour. Worth trying in lamb stews, too.*

Preheat the oven to 180°C/350°F/gas mark 4.

Rub the chicken all over with olive oil and plenty of salt and pepper.

Put all the ingredients, except the cream, pastry and egg, into a large casserole dish. Put the lid on and place in the oven for 1½–2 hours, until the chicken is falling off the bone. (Check now and then and add a dash of water if it seems dry.)

Leave the chicken until cool enough to handle. Pick off the meat and put it into a pie dish with the vegetables and juice from the casserole, discarding only the skin, bones and bay leaves. Stir in the cream. Season. You can put this into the fridge now until you want to make the pie (several days later, if you fancy).

When the filling has cooled completely and you are ready to cook the pie, heat the oven to 160°C/325°F/gas mark 3. Roll out the pastry to make the lid, and use the trimmings to cut out a decoration for the top. I like to write the word 'Pie'. Glaze with the beaten egg.

Cook the pie for 40 minutes or until the top is golden.

# FRENCH ONION TART

**SERVES: 8 AS A CANAPÉ OR 4 FOR LUNCH**
**PREP TIME: 30 MINS + RESTING · COOK TIME: 30 MINS**

## SPELT PASTRY:

125g **plain spelt flour**

a pinch of **salt**

a pinch of **sugar**

100g cold **unsalted butter**, cut into pieces, plus extra for greasing

4 tablespoons **iced water**

## TOPPING:

3 tablespoons **olive oil**

2 **onions**, thinly sliced

1 teaspoon **vinegar**

small bunch of **thyme**

50g **black** or **niçoise olives**

6 **salted anchovy fillets**

1 **free-range egg**, beaten

**salt** and **black pepper**

## ≡ ALTERNATIVE TOPPINGS ≡

- Onions, slices of buffalo mozzarella and tomato, basil. Drizzle of olive oil.
- Onions, sausage, chopped sage.
- Fine layer of Dijon mustard, onions, slices of tomato, thyme.
- Onions, small pieces of broccoli. Add goats' cheese after cooking.

*This recipe is an adaptation of the French classic pissaladière, made with spelt flour. It is very simple and the possibilities for toppings are endless.*

The spelt pastry: Combine the spelt flour, salt and sugar in a bowl and cut in the butter with a knife. Leave larger chunks of butter than you would think (about the size of a garlic clove) to make the pastry more flaky.

Drizzle in the water and bring it all together in a ball.

Wrap in clingfilm, and let it rest in the fridge for at least 30 minutes.

The topping: Heat the oil in a heavy-based saucepan and add the sliced onions. Cook for 7–8 minutes, stirring occasionally to be sure they don't burn. You are looking for a caramelized but soft onion.

Once cooked, add the vinegar and 2 teaspoons of water. Sprinkle with thyme leaves and transfer into a bowl to cool.

Heat the oven to 160°C/325°F/gas mark 3 and grease a baking tray.

Pit and break up the olives a little. On a floured surface, roll out the dough to approximately 3mm thick and transfer to the baking tray. Arrange the cooled onions, anchovies and olives over the dough, leaving a small border, and season with salt and pepper.

Brush the edges with beaten egg, then bake in the oven for 25–30 minutes until golden and crisp.

# ESTHER'S PORK PIE

MAKES: 1 LARGE PORK PIE

PREP TIME: 1 HOUR + CHILLING AND COOLING · COOK TIME: 1¾ HOURS

40g **butter**, diced, plus extra for greasing

60g **lard**, diced

100ml **water**

275g **plain flour**, plus extra for dusting

¾ teaspoon **salt**

1 **free-range egg**, beaten, plus extra
beaten egg for brushing

500g **pork shoulder** or **leg**

250g **pork belly**

250g **bacon**

**salt**, **pepper**, **thyme**, **mace**, **chilli**, or
any other seasoning you like

600ml warm **stock**

30g **powdered beef gelatine** (I use
Dr Oetker's)

*This recipe is a favourite of Esther Walker, a friend of Henry's. A classic pie – perfect for picnics.*

Heat the butter, lard and water in a saucepan until it is melted and warm, but don't let it boil. While the fat is melting, put the flour and salt into a mixing bowl and make a well in the centre. Pour the egg into the well and half mix it in with a knife. Once the fat and water have melted together, add to the flour and mix until it forms a dough.

The dough will probably be a bit too sticky, so sprinkle on more flour until it takes on the glossy sheen of pastry. Form it into a ball, wrap it in clingfilm and chill in the fridge for an hour.

When you take it out of the fridge you can cut off a quarter to put aside for the lid – but I find that if you are using a pie tin (15–17cm in diameter and 15cm deep) it's easier to roll the whole lot out on a lightly floured surface, lay it over and press it into the greased pie tin, then cut off the excess and re-roll that to make the lid.

Don't be afraid to make the walls of the pie really quite thick – up to 1cm or more. The crust is just a vessel for the pork inside; it's going to have to be robust enough to contain hot pork fat AND the warm jellied stock you are going to pour in later. If it's a dainty 0.5cm thick, it will tear on cooking.

Heat your oven to 180°C/350°F/gas mark 4. Mince the pork and bacon quite finely in a food processor. Sort through the meat after it's been processed to pick out any bits of gristle or rind.

Add salt, pepper, thyme, mace, chilli or anything else you'd like to the filling and mix in well. You can test the filling's seasoning by frying a small piece and tasting.

Fill your pastry-lined pie dish with the pork filling, really ramming in as much as you can. However much you stuff it, it will all shrink on cooking, so don't be afraid to squash in as much as possible, pummelling it all in, like punching a sleeping bag back into its carry-case.

Now roll out your remaining pastry to make the pie lid. You must, must brush beaten egg round the top edges of the pie to seal the lid to the sides. Nothing else will do: if you use anything else, the lid will come away from the sides and stuff will fall out and it'll just be a disaster.

Lay the lid on top of the pie and press it all around the edges to seal. Trim away the excess pastry round the sides.

On the top of the pie, in the centre, make a good, generous hole in the pastry, about the width of your little finger. This is so that juices can escape during cooking and for pouring in the stock at the end.

Brush the lid with more beaten egg and shove it in the oven for 30 minutes. Then turn the heat down to 160°C/325°F/gas mark 3 and cook for another 1¼ hours.

Leave the pie in the tin to get cool all the way through – this might take 4 or 5 hours. During cooking, the pork will have shrunk away from the sides of the pastry to form a natural cavity to be filled by the jelly.

RECIPE CONTINUES ⟶

You can make the jelly in two ways: the first of these is to make up 600ml of warm stock – any sort will do, even from a stock cube – and set it with powdered gelatine. I find Dr Oetker's powdered beef gelatine to be the most user-friendly. One 30g sachet sets 600ml of stock. The second, if you're feeling very serious, is to ask your butcher for some veal bones or a pig's trotter. Boil them in water for a couple of hours with some carrots and celery and the stock will turn to jelly when it sets, without needing the help of manufactured gelatine.

Pour the jelly stock through the hole in the top of the pie while the stock is still lukewarm, and it will set around the pork as it cools. This is quite a tricky process. You can use a turkey baster if you've got one, or a jug and funnel. Don't lose heart if the stock bubbles out of your pie's blowhole and goes everywhere. This kind of pastry is pretty resilient. You may have to repeat the pouring-in of the stock after you've poured in the first lot, as it will slowly disappear into the nooks and crannies of the pie and suddenly there will be a 1cm gap between the lid of the pie and the top of the jelly. Chill the pie in the fridge for at least an hour before eating.

# CHEESE EMPANADAS

MAKES: 20 SMALL EMPANADAS
PREP TIME: 30 MINS + RESTING · COOK TIME: 10–15 MINS
V

400g **plain flour**, plus extra for dusting

2 teaspoons **baking powder**

1 teaspoon **salt**

115g **butter**

50ml **orange juice**

80ml **sparkling water**

250g **mozzarella cheese**

1 **onion**, grated or finely chopped

1½–2 tablespoons **caster sugar**, plus extra to sprinkle (optional)

1 **free-range egg**, lightly beaten

**vegetable oil**, for frying (optional)

*These are great for parties as they can be made ahead of time.*

Put the flour, baking powder and salt into a food processor and whizz until well mixed.

Add the butter, orange juice and sparkling water and process until a dough forms.

Tip the dough on to a surface, bring it together into a ball, wrap it in clingfilm and place in the fridge for 30 minutes to rest.

Grate the mozzarella into a bowl and add the onion. Add the sugar and mix well.

Preheat the oven to 200°C/400°F/gas mark 6. Line a baking tray with baking paper.

When the dough has rested, remove it from the clingfilm and dust your work surface with flour. Cut the ball of dough in half (it's easier to roll out smaller amounts). Roll out the dough so that it's only a couple of millimetres thick.

Using a 9–10cm cutter, cut circles out of the dough. Place a teaspoon of the cheese filling in the centre of each circle, fold the dough over to make a halfmoon shape, and seal the edges by pressing down with a fork. Make sure they are all well sealed, otherwise the filling will ooze out when you cook them.

Brush the empanadas with the beaten egg, and sprinkle a little sugar over the top of each one if you want that extra sweetness. Place on the baking tray and cook in the oven for 10–15 minutes, until golden. Cool on a wire rack.

If you fancy them fried, fill a saucepan 3–4cm deep with vegetable oil. Heat the oil and deep-fry the empanadas for about 2 minutes on each side or until golden. Sprinkle with caster sugar before serving.

# GLENYS'S DESPERATE DAN STEAK PIE

SERVES: 6
PREP TIME: 20 MINS + COOLING · COOK TIME: 2¾ HOURS

olive oil or **vegetable oil**

1.3kg **beef steak**, diced

6 **onions**, chopped

8 **bay leaves**

900ml **Newcastle Brown Ale**, or a similar sweet ale

**sea salt** and freshly ground **black pepper**

1 x 375g packet of **ready-rolled puff pastry** (or **flaky pastry** from page 212)

1 **free-range egg**, beaten, for glazing

**TO SERVE:**

boiled **potatoes** (optional)

wilted **greens** (optional)

*Henry's next-door neighbour, Glenys, serves this simple old-fashioned pie to Andy (her man) when she wants to treat him right.*

Heat the oven to 160°C/325°F/gas mark 3.

Heat a dash of oil in a large casserole dish. Add the beef, brown on all sides and set aside – you might need to do this in batches to make sure it browns well.

Add a dash more oil to the casserole, add the onions and cook until golden. Add the bay leaves and return the meat to the casserole. Add the ale and season well with salt and pepper.

Cook in the oven for 2 hours, stirring every 45 minutes or so and checking that it hasn't dried out. You can add more ale if necessary.

When the meat is tender, allow to cool and taste for seasoning.

When you are ready to assemble the pie, heat the oven to 160°C/325°F/gas mark 3. Transfer the cooled meat mixture to a pie dish and top with the rolled puff pastry. Press the pastry around the rim to seal. If you are feeling creative, try making shapes from the leftover bits of pastry. The children can help.

Glaze the top of the pastry with the beaten egg, using a pastry brush, and make a hole in the middle to allow steam to escape. Bake for 40 minutes, or until the pastry is golden and you can see the juices bubbling up. Serve with boiled potatoes and wilted greens.

## ═ TIP ═

You can make the beef and ale filling well in advance of assembling it with the pastry, or double up on quantities and freeze half. Then you only need to defrost it if you want to make the pie in a hurry.

# SALMON & DILL MUFFINS

MAKES: 6

PREP TIME: 15 MINS · COOK TIME: 20 MINS

240g **plain flour**

2 teaspoons **baking powder**

165g **grated cheese**

50g **smoked salmon**, chopped

20g **fresh dill**, chopped

1 **free-range egg**

180ml **buttermilk**

75ml **vegetable** or **sunflower oil**

100g **cream cheese**

*A savoury breakfast muffin.*

Heat the oven to 180°/350°F/gas mark 4, and line a 6-hole muffin tin with paper cases.

Mix the flour and baking powder together in a large bowl. Add the grated cheese, smoked salmon and dill.

In a separate bowl beat together the egg, buttermilk and oil.

Place half the wet ingredients into the dry ingredients and stir well. Then add the rest of the wet ingredients and mix until completely combined.

Spoon into the muffin cases until each is half full, then place a heaped teaspoon of cream cheese in the middle of each muffin. Top them up until they are full with the muffin mixture.

Cook for 10 minutes, then take the tin out and turn it around so the muffins cook evenly. Put the tin back into the oven and continue to cook for a further 10 minutes, or until the muffins are just browning on top.

# SWEET PIES
# & PASTRIES

# LEON PECAN PIE

SERVES: 8–10

PREP TIME: 30 MINS + CHILLING · COOK TIME: 1 HOUR 10 MINS

WF · GF · V

150g **butter**, plus extra for greasing

100g **caster sugar**

1 **free-range egg**, plus 1 **yolk**

270g **gluten-free plain flour**, plus extra
    for dusting

**FILLING:**

50g **butter**

225g **golden syrup**

2 tablespoons **caster sugar**

1 teaspoon **cornflour**

2 large **free-range eggs**

200g **pecan nut halves**

*A simple, rich, gluten-free pecan tart that was a staple in our restaurant
for years. Baked by Craig Barton, one of our favourite bakers.*

For the pastry, cream together the butter and sugar with a wooden spoon or in
a free-standing electric mixer until smooth.

Add the egg and egg yolk and mix until fully incorporated. Add the flour and quickly
bring it together in a ball. Wrap the pastry tightly in clingfilm and refrigerate for at
least 30 minutes.

Grease a 23–25cm fluted flan tin. Roll the pastry out on a floured surface to about
3–5mm thick and line your tart tin with it. Trim the edges and chill in the fridge for
30 minutes. Meanwhile, heat the oven to 160°C/325°F/gas mark 3.

Line the chilled pastry case with baking paper, and fill it with baking beans to stop
it shrinking while it's being baked. Bake in the oven for 20 minutes then remove the
baking beans and paper. Return to the oven and bake for a further 5 minutes. The
pastry should be a nice blonde colour. Set aside to cool.

Put the butter and golden syrup into a medium saucepan over a low heat. When it becomes runny, take it off the heat and whisk in the sugar. Allow to cool a little.

In a small bowl, whisk the cornflour and eggs until smooth and add to the saucepan.

Fill the baked pastry with the pecan halves. Pour the golden syrup mixture on top and fill it up to just below the edge of the case. Put into the oven, taking great care not to spill any liquid over the sides, as this might make it difficult to remove it from the tin once it's baked.

Bake for about 40 minutes, or until the tart is a dark golden colour and has slightly risen in the middle. Take out of the oven and leave to cool in the tin.

≡ TIP ≡

This can be served cold for tea, or warm with ice cream.

PICTURED OVERLEAF ⟶

# DITTISHAM PLUM CRUMBLE

SERVES: 6
PREP TIME: 15 MINS · COOK TIME: 45 MINS
WF · GF · V

1kg tart **plums** (Dittisham or Marjorie
    are good)
50g **caster sugar**
3 tablespoons **gluten-free plain flour**
1 tablespoon **sweet white wine**

**CRUMBLE TOPPING:**
100g **gluten-free plain flour**
100g **ground almonds**
50g **flaked almonds**
85g **brown sugar**
a pinch of **sea salt**
¼ teaspoon **ground cinnamon**
150g cold **unsalted butter**, cut into
    1cm cubes

*Crumbles are all about getting the balance right between sweet and sour and soft and crisp. This makes a lovely conclusion to a simple summer supper.*

Heat the oven to 180°C/350°F/gas mark 4.

Halve and stone the plums and place in a bowl. Toss with the sugar, flour and wine and put into a deep 23–25cm baking dish.

Put all the crumble topping ingredients into a bowl and use the back of a fork or two knives to break up the chunks of butter into tiny pieces.

Scatter the topping lightly over the fruit and place in the oven.

Bake for 40–45 minutes, or until the fruit is bubbling and the topping is golden.

## ═ TIP ═
Almonds and plums go nicely together here, but you could substitute hazelnuts and blueberries, or walnuts and apples.

# KEY LIME PIE

SERVES: 6–8

PREP TIME: 20 MINS · COOK TIME: 25–35 MINS

V

200g crushed **digestive biscuits**

85g **unsalted butter**, melted

400g **sweetened condensed milk**

4 large **free-range egg yolks**

1 tablespoon **lime zest**, plus extra for garnish (about 3 limes)

120ml freshly squeezed **lime juice**

350ml **double cream**, chilled

≡ TIP ≡

It is possible to buy digestive biscuits already crushed if you frequent a certain kind of cash-and-carry. Otherwise, simply put the biscuits into a thick plastic bag and smash them with a rolling pin.

*Key limes come from the Florida Keys (hence the name) and tend to be smaller and sweeter than conventional limes. If you can't get to Florida for your groceries, don't worry – the flavour will still be wonderful.*

Heat the oven to 180°C/350°F/gas mark 4.

Combine the crushed digestive biscuits and melted butter in a medium bowl and mix well. Press the mixture into a 23cm pie plate and bake in the oven until lightly browned. This will take about 12–15 minutes. Remove from the oven and transfer the pie plate to a wire rack until completely cooled.

Lower the oven to 160°C/325°F/gas mark 3.

In a medium bowl, gently whisk together the condensed milk, egg yolks, lime zest and juice. Pour into the prepared, cooled crust.

Return the pie to the oven and bake until the centre is set but still quivers when the pan is nudged. This should take 15–20 minutes.

Let the pie cool completely in the tin on top of a wire rack.

Once the pie has cooled, place it in the fridge to chill until ready to serve.

Before serving, lightly whip the cream into soft peaks. Spread the cream over the chilled pie. Garnish with a little more lime zest.

# STRAWBERRY & BLUEBERRY COBBLER

SERVES: 6

PREP TIME: 15 MINS + RESTING · COOK TIME: 40 MINS

WF · GF · V

250g **blueberries**

500g **strawberries**, hulled and quartered

50g **caster sugar**

4 tablespoons **cornflour**

200g **gluten-free self-raising flour**

2 teaspoons **gluten-free baking powder**

a large pinch of **salt**

50g **unsalted butter**, cut into small cubes

150ml **double cream**, plus extra
   for brushing

*Cobblers are the perfect summer pudding. (In fact, they make a damned good summer Sunday breakfast.) The cobbler topping is like a scone or American biscuit and melts into the jammy fruit. Serve this one with thick cream.*

Heat the oven to 180°C/350°F/gas mark 4.

Combine the berries, sugar and cornflour and put into a deep 1–1.5 litre baking dish.

Put the flour, baking powder, salt and butter into a bowl and use the back of a fork or two knives to break up the chunks of butter into tiny pieces. Pour over the cream and mix until it all comes together.

Press the topping into a ball and place on a floured work surface. Let the mixture rest for 10 minutes. Then roll the dough out to a 2cm thickness and cut out circles with a biscuit cutter.

Lay the circles flat over the fruit, brush with extra cream and place on a baking tray to catch any drips.

Bake in the oven for 35–40 minutes, or until the fruit is bubbling and the topping is golden brown.

## ≡ TIPS ≡

You can also make this cobbler topping with regular self-raising flour.

Experiment with different fruits: peaches and nectarines work well, with a little added lemon zest and juice.

# HATTIE'S BLACKCURRANT TART CANELLE

SERVES: 6–8
PREP TIME: 25 MINS + CHILLING · COOK TIME: 25 MINS
V

170g **plain flour**, plus extra for dusting
85g **unsalted butter**, plus extra for greasing
85g **caster sugar**, plus extra for sprinkling
2 **free-range egg yolks**
1 tablespoon **water**
1 level tablespoon **ground cinnamon**
**vanilla ice cream** or **crème fraîche**,
     to serve

**FILLING:**
225g **blackcurrants**, off the stalk
extra **caster sugar** to add to the currants
**milk** or **beaten egg**, to glaze

Preheat the oven to 180°C/350°F/gas mark 4 and grease an 18cm fluted flan tin.

To make the pastry in a food processor, put in the flour, butter, sugar, egg yolks, water and cinnamon and blitz until it comes together into a ball. Remove from the machine, cover with clingfilm and chill well for at least an hour in the fridge.

To make the pastry by hand, rub together the flour, butter, sugar and cinnamon with your fingers until you have a breadcrumb-like consistency. Slowly add the egg yolks and water until the mixture comes together into a ball. Cover with clingfilm and chill well.

Put the blackcurrants into a pan, cover generously with caster sugar, and put over a low heat. Stir regularly, and when you are sure that all the sugar has dissolved, turn up the heat until the fruit is bubbling and thickened. Remove from the heat.

Roll out the pastry on a floured surface to 1cm thick and line the flan tin, gathering up any trimmings. Fill the flan case with the blackcurrant compote, and roll out the trimmings to make a thin and neat extra strip to go around the edge. There should be enough pastry left to make a lattice pattern over the top of the tart if you wish.

Brush the pastry with milk or beaten egg, and bake in the oven for 20–25 minutes, until the pastry is golden. Serve cool, with vanilla ice cream or crème fraîche.

# MAGGIE'S CROATIAN PEAR PIE

SERVES: 4–6

PREP TIME: 50 MINS · COOK TIME: ABOUT 45 MINS

V

175g **caster sugar** or **soft brown sugar**

125g **unsalted butter**, plus extra
   for greasing

375g **plain flour**, plus extra for dusting

1 **free-range egg**

¼ teaspoon **baking powder**

a pinch of **salt**

4–6 ripe **pears**

100g **apricot jam**

**cream** or **vanilla ice cream**, to serve
   (optional)

**ALMOND FILLING:**

200g **unsalted butter**, softened

200g **icing sugar**

2 **free-range eggs**, plus 2 **yolks**

a dash of **Calvados** (optional),
   or other alcohol

200g **ground almonds**

60g **plain flour**

*This pie can be done in a square, oval, loaf or any shape tin you fancy. Also, the pears can be cut into halves, quarters or slices, depending on the look you like.*

Heat the oven to 220°C/425°F/gas mark 7 and grease a 25cm tart tin.

To make the pastry, beat together the sugar and butter, until you get a smooth paste. Add the flour, egg, baking powder and salt and mix well, adding a little water if you need to. The pastry will be very crumbly, but do not despair, it's supposed to be like that.

Roll out the pastry on a floured surface and line the tart tin, pricking it all over with a fork. If the pastry is too crumbly, press it into the tin by hand a little at a time. It should have a thick crust of pastry, so don't be alarmed by the amount you have. Line it with baking paper and fill with baking beans. Blind bake for 8–10 minutes, depending on your oven, then remove the paper and beans and allow it to cool.

Reduce the oven temperature to 180°C/350°F/gas mark 4.

Peel the pears, leaving the stalks on. Cut them into slices or halve them, removing the core carefully so they don't break.

To make the almond filling, cream together the butter and sugar, then add the eggs and egg yolks one at a time, mixing after each addition. You can do this by hand or using an electric hand mixer. Add the alcohol if you are using it, then the ground almonds and flour, and mix well.

Pour the filling into the pastry base, and arrange the pears on top, any which way you like.

Bake the pie in the oven for 30–40 minutes, or until golden brown, but do not let it burn. Allow to cool in the tin.

Heat the apricot jam in a small pan with a teaspoon or two of water until it is runny and spreadable, and whilst still warm, use a pastry brush to glaze your pie. Eat this pie lukewarm on its own, with cream or a good vanilla ice cream.

=≡ TIP ≡=

If you are making this in a loaf tin, bake for a further 20 minutes on a low oven shelf.

PICTURED OVERLEAF ⟶

# APPLE CRISP

**SERVES: 6**

**PREP TIME: 20 MINS · COOK TIME: 35 MINS**

**V** (**GF** if gluten-free bread is used)

1.5kg **apples**, peeled, quartered
and cored

juice of 1 **lemon**

75g **caster sugar**, plus an extra
2 tablespoons for sprinkling

¼ teaspoon **ground cinnamon**

200g stale, **crusty white bread**,
crusts removed, torn into pieces

100g **salted butter**, melted

**pouring cream**, to serve

*A very easy pudding, and a great way to turn your stale bread into something delicious and sumptuous.*

Heat the oven to 180°C/350°F/gas mark 4.

Combine the apples, lemon juice, sugar and cinnamon and put into a deep 1–1.5 litre baking dish.

In a bowl, toss the bread pieces in the melted butter and then arrange in a layer over the apples. Sprinkle sugar over the top and place on a baking tray to catch any drips.

Bake in the oven for 30–35 minutes, or until the fruit is bubbling and the topping is golden. Serve hot with pouring cream.

## ≡ TIPS ≡

Try using pears instead of apples and add a splash of white wine.

Don't use sourdough or levain bread because it will be too sour. Use plain white bread or a French stick or baguette, nice and stale.

# JANET'S LONDON FIELDS
# APRICOT & CHERRY GALETTE

SERVES 6–8

PREP TIME: 30 MINS + CHILLING · COOK TIME: 45–50 MINS

V

2 tablespoons **sugar**

1 tablespoon **plain flour**

1 tablespoon **ground almonds** (optional)

450g fresh **apricots**, washed, halved
and pitted

225g **cherries**, washed and pitted

1 **free-range egg**, beaten

**vanilla ice cream** or **whipped cream**,
to serve (optional)

**PASTRY:**

125g **plain flour**, plus extra for dusting

a pinch of **salt**

a pinch of **sugar**

85g cold **unsalted butter**, cut into
1.5cm pieces

4 tablespoons **ice-cold water**

## ≡ TIP ≡

This is basically a free-form, open-
face tart and it can be used for all
different kinds of fruit.

For the pastry, combine the flour, salt and sugar in a bowl and either cut in the cold butter with the back of a fork or use two knives.

Avoid overmixing – leaving larger chunks of butter than you would expect will make the pastry more flaky. Drizzle in the water and bring it all together into a ball without working the dough. Wrap in clingfilm, then flatten into a disc and let it rest in the fridge for about 45 minutes.

Heat the oven to 200°C/400°F/gas mark 6 and line a baking tray with baking paper. Allow the pastry to come to room temperature so it's easier to work.

Dust a work surface with flour and roll out the dough into a circle about the size of a dinner plate. Put it on the baking tray and return it to the fridge for a few minutes.

Remove the pastry circle from the fridge and sprinkle the sugar, flour and ground almonds over, leaving a 2–3cm border around the outside. Arrange the fruit on top of the almonds – you can put the cherries in the middle and the apricots in a circle around them, or make up your own pattern.

Fold over the pastry rim to create a crust. Brush the rim with beaten egg, and bake in the bottom half of the oven for 45–50 minutes, until the fruit is squashy.

When cooked, transfer the galette to a wire rack to cool.

Serve warm or cold, with vanilla ice cream or whipped cream. Or simply enjoy it on its own with a cup of tea.

# ANDI'S MARSHMALLOW-TOPPED SWEET POTATO PIE

. . . . . . . . . . . . . . . . . . . . . . . . . . . . . . . . . . . . . . . . . . . . . . . . . . . . .

**SERVES: 6–8**
**PREP TIME: 25 MINS · COOK TIME: 50 MINS**
**V**

. . . . . . . . . . . . . . . . . . . . . . . . . . . . . . . . . . . . . . . . . . . . . . . . . . . . .

**flour**, for dusting

**butter**, for greasing

1 x 375g packet of **sweet shortcrust pastry**

4 **pink-fleshed sweet potatoes**

6 tablespoons of **honey**, **agave nectar** or any sweetener that you prefer

1 teaspoon **ground nutmeg**

1 teaspoon **ground cinnamon**

1 teaspoon **ground allspice**

1 teaspoon **vanilla extract**

2 tablespoons **desiccated coconut** (optional)

3 **free-range egg whites**

1 packet of **white mini marshmallows**

Preheat the oven to 180°C/350°F/gas mark 4 and grease a 25–28cm fluted flan tin.

Roll out the pastry on a floured work surface and use to line the flan tin measuring about 25–28cm. Line pastry case with baking paper, and fill it with baking beans to stop it shrinking while it's being baked. Bake in the oven for 25 minutes, until the pastry is golden, then remove from the oven, take out the baking beans and paper and set aside to cool, leaving the oven on.

Meanwhile, peel the sweet potatoes and cut them into cubes. Boil until soft, then drain and mash them well.

Put the sweet potatoes into a large bowl with the honey, nutmeg, cinnamon, allspice, vanilla extract and the coconut (if using). Mix thoroughly.

Beat the egg whites well in a separate bowl, then add to the sweet potatoes and whip the mixture together for a few minutes. Pour into the pastry case and bake in the oven for around 20 minutes, until the top of the pie has a few browned peaks.

Gently arrange the marshmallows on top in any design that you like.

When you are ready to eat the pie, place it under a hot grill to toast the marshmallows, which will go golden and start to melt very quickly. Keep a close eye on it so that they don't burn. Serve immediately.

# PUMPKIN PIE

SERVES: 8–10

PREP TIME: 25 MINS · COOK TIME: 35 MINS

V

450g **pumpkin purée** (bought or homemade – see tip)

3 **free-range eggs**

100ml **double cream**

150g **light brown sugar**

1 teaspoon **ground cinnamon**

½ teaspoon **ground ginger**

½ teaspoon **ground star anise**

½ teaspoon **ground allspice**

1 teaspoon **sea salt**

3 tablespoons **maple syrup**

finely grated **fresh ginger** (optional)

**black pepper** (optional)

1 x quantity **Shortcrust Pastry** (see page 212) or 250g ready-made **sweet shortcrust pastry**

**flour**, for dusting

**butter**, for greasing

**Chantilly cream**, to serve

*A warm, deeply spicy version of this Thanksgiving classic.*

Heat the oven to 180°C/350°F/gas mark 4 and grease a 23cm fluted flan tin with a loose bottom.

Whisk all the ingredients together, except the ginger, pepper and pastry, in a large bowl. The pie will be silkier if the pumpkin is as smooth as possible, so push the filling through a fine strainer.

Taste the filling. At this point, you can add a little finely grated fresh ginger, along with a good grinding of black pepper to taste, if you like.

Roll out the pastry on a lightly floured surface as thinly as possible and press into the flan tin, then trim the edges. Pour the filling into the pastry case and bake in the oven for about 35 minutes, or until the custardy filling is just set while retaining a slight wobble.

Cool and serve with lots of Chantilly cream (double cream sweetened with caster sugar and a dash of vanilla extract).

## ≡ TIP ≡

To make your own purée, cut a small cooking pumpkin in half, remove the seeds and bake it in a hot oven, cut side down. When it is soft, scrape out the flesh and purée. If the pumpkins are not as sweet as you'd like, use some freshly puréed butternut squash as well.

# CLAIRE'S CHERRY PIE

SERVES 8
PREP TIME: 40 MINS · COOK TIME: 1 HOUR
V

butter, for greasing

350g **Shortcrust Pastry** (see page 212)

500g fresh or frozen pitted **sour cherries**, preferably Morello

200g **caster sugar**

4 tablespoons **cornflour**

a pinch of **salt**

1 **free-range egg**

a little **milk**

*Sour cherries are a favourite pie filling in America. They grow in the UK in many back gardens, but are rarely found in supermarkets as they don't travel well. If you can't find fresh cherries, use frozen or preserved ones.*

Heat the oven to 200°C/400°F/gas mark 6 and grease a 20–23cm pie dish or fluted tart tin.

Roll out half of the pastry into a disc large enough to line the pie dish with some excess. Place the disc of pastry in the dish, pressing down well. Roll the other half of the pastry into a rectangle 3mm thick and place it on a baking tray lined with baking paper. Place both in the fridge while you prepare the filling.

Put the cherries, sugar and cornflour into a bowl and add the salt. Toss to coat the fruit evenly.

Remove the pie dish from the fridge and fill it with the cherry mixture. Remove the rectangle of pastry from the fridge and use a small knife to slice the pastry into 2cm strips. Arrange the strips of pastry over the cherries in a lattice pattern.

Crack the egg into a small bowl and add a few drops of milk. Whisk to combine. Trim the edges of the pastry to the rim of the dish. Using a pastry brush, carefully coat the lattice with egg wash.

Place the pie in the oven for about an hour, with a piece of kitchen foil underneath to catch any drips. The pie is ready when you see the fruit filling bubbling through.

# TARTE TATIN

SERVES: 8

PREP TIME: 35 MINS · COOK TIME: 40 MINS

V

250g ready-made **puff pastry**

**flour**, for dusting

4–6 medium **apples** (Cox's and Granny
Smiths are good)

juice of ½ **lemon**

25g **unsalted butter**

75g **caster sugar**

**pouring cream**, to serve

*Crisp pastry and warm, soft caramelized apples in a pool of cream.*

Heat the oven to 200°C/400°F/gas mark 6. Line a baking tray with baking paper.

On a lightly floured surface, roll the pastry into a 30cm disc. Use a sharp knife to carefully trim the edge, making as perfect a disc as you can without losing too much of the diameter. Place the pastry circle carefully on the lined baking tray. Place it in the freezer if it will fit; if not, place it in the fridge.

Peel, quarter and core the apples, then coat in the lemon juice.

Place a 25–30cm tatin dish – or a medium ovenproof frying pan – on a medium heat, and melt the butter until it foams. Add the sugar and allow it to dissolve. Turn up the heat and continue to cook until the sugar just starts to caramelize (goes light brown). Remove from the heat. The caramel will continue to darken as it cools, so take it off the heat well before it reaches a dark caramel.

Arrange the apples tightly in the pan in 2 layers.

Place the chilled circle of pastry over the top of the pan and tuck the edges down inside. Pierce the pastry with a knife to allow steam to escape during baking.

Place the pan in the oven and bake for about 30 minutes, until the pastry is golden and the juices are bubbling. Remove from the oven and allow to rest for 5 minutes.

Run a small knife around the edge of the pan to release the tart. Place a serving plate slightly larger than the tart pan over the tart, and carefully flip the tart over on to the plate. Drizzle any juices over the tart then serve hot with plenty of pouring cream.

## ≡ TIPS ≡

If you are unsure about when to stop cooking the caramel, you can take it as dark as you like it and then stop the cooking process by dunking the bottom of the pan in a sink full of ice-cold water. This will arrest the cooking so that the caramel does not burn.

Try swapping the apples for pears or quinces.

# CAKES

# SIMNEL CAKE

SERVES: 10–12

PREP TIME: 1 HOUR · COOK TIME: 3½ HOURS

V

225g **plain flour**

½ teaspoon **salt**

¼ teaspoon freshly grated **nutmeg**

½ teaspoon **ground cinnamon**

¼ teaspoon **allspice**

175g **unsalted butter**, plus extra
  for greasing

175g **demerara sugar**

2 tablespoons **dark treacle** or **molasses**

3 **free-range eggs**, plus extra to glaze

450g **currants**

300g **sultanas**

120g good-quality **candied peel**

zest and juice of 1 **lemon**

50g **ground almonds**

150ml **whole milk**

a little **apricot jam**

**MARZIPAN:**

450g **icing sugar**

450g **ground almonds**

2 **free-range eggs**

1 teaspoon **lemon juice**

1 teaspoon **almond extract**

*Petra is Henry's mother-in-law. Simnel cake is a British Easter tradition. It is widely accepted that the balls of marzipan on top are meant to represent the disciples, but there is some debate as to how many there should be: 11 if you exclude the traitor Judas, 12 if you count him in or 13 to include Jesus. Petra's homemade marzipan is so good that we recommend 13: every time you leave the room you will return to find that another ball has mysteriously vanished.*

First make the marzipan. Sift the icing sugar into a bowl, then add the ground almonds, eggs, lemon juice and almond extract to taste. Add the extract slowly, and keep tasting as some brands are stronger than others. Form into a ball and knead lightly. Divide into 3 pieces and wrap each one tightly in clingfilm until ready to use.

Heat the oven to 150°C/300°F/gas mark 2. Grease and line a deep 20cm cake tin with baking paper.

Sift the flour, salt and spices together and set aside.

In another bowl, cream the butter, sugar and black treacle or molasses until very light and fluffy. Add the eggs one at a time, sprinkling in a little of the sifted flour and beating well after each addition. Stir in the remaining flour, then the fruit, peel, zest, juice and ground almonds. Add the milk and mix until all the ingredients are well combined.

Roll out one of the pieces of marzipan into a 20cm disc. Turn half the cake mixture into the tin, level it out and cover it with this disc of marzipan. Then cover with the rest of the cake mixture and smooth the top.

Bake in the oven for about 3½ hours, or until a skewer inserted into the centre of the cake comes out clean. The top of the cake should be dull, not shiny.

When the cake is completely cooled, brush the top with a little warmed jam, sieved if necessary. Roll out another ball of marzipan and place it on top of the cake, pressing it down well. Score the top in a cross-hatch pattern. Brush with a little lightly beaten egg.

Turn the grill or oven to high. Divide the remaining ball of marzipan into 11, 12 or 13 balls, as you wish, and arrange them round the edge of the cake. Brush each ball with egg and put the cake into the oven or under the grill for a few minutes to give it that attractive, toasted appearance.

## ═ TIPS ═

Petra says the bore of Simnel cake is twiggy currants. She always picks them over to remove the little twigs.

If your oven runs hot, wrap a second layer of paper around the outside of the cake tin to keep it from getting too dark.

If you are serving the cake to the infirm, try to find pasteurized eggs – or eggs from flocks you trust (the ones with Lion marks are good) – for making the marzipan.

PICTURED OVERLEAF ⟶

# LIFE BY CHOCOLATE CAKE

SERVES: 10–12

PREP TIME: 20 MINS · COOK TIME: 45–50 MINS

WF · GF · V

5 **free-range eggs**

200g soft **light brown sugar**

100ml **instant espresso**

350g **dark chocolate**, broken into pieces

250g **unsalted butter**, cut into small pieces

1 teaspoon **vanilla extract**

a pinch of **sea salt**

*This flourless chocolate cake is SO rich, yet super-light, like a mousse. Once you have made it once, you will make it again and again, not least because your friends and family will give you no choice. You have been warned.*

Heat the oven to 160°C/325°F/gas mark 3. Butter a 23cm cake tin, preferably not one with a loose bottom, and line the base and sides with baking paper.

With an electric hand mixer, beat the eggs and 100g of the sugar until the mixture forms voluminous peaks.

In a saucepan, dissolve the remaining sugar in the coffee over a medium heat, then stir in the chocolate pieces and butter and take off the heat.

Add the vanilla and salt to the saucepan and stir occasionally until everything is completely melted.

In a steady stream, pour the melted chocolate mixture into the whisked eggs and stir just until combined.

Pour into the prepared cake tin, then place in a deep roasting tin and pour enough hot water into the roasting tin to reach almost to the top of the cake tin.

Bake in the oven for 45–50 minutes. The cake should be set but not solid. Leave to cool in the tin.

## ⹀ TIP ⹀

This cake tastes even more beautiful with a little dollop of crème fraîche.

# CLEMENTINE POLENTA CAKE

SERVES: 12

PREP TIME: 25 MINS + COOLING · COOK TIME: 50 MINS

WF · GF · V

250g **unsalted butter**, very soft, plus
extra for greasing

250g **caster sugar**

2 **free-range eggs**

200g **fine polenta**

100g **ground almonds**

1 teaspoon **gluten-free baking powder**

zest and juice of 3 **clementines**

2 tablespoons **lemon juice**

**Greek yoghurt** or **double cream**, to serve

**SYRUP:**

50ml **runny honey**

juice of 1 **clementine** and 1 **lemon**

*This moist flourless cake is perfect for teatime, but also makes a beautiful pudding when drizzled with a little cream or topped with a blob of yoghurt.*

Heat the oven to 170°C/340°F/gas mark 3½. Grease a 25cm round cake tin and line it with baking paper.

In a large mixing bowl, beat the soft butter and sugar until very pale and fluffy. Add the eggs one at a time, beating well after each addition.

In a separate bowl, whisk together by hand the polenta, ground almonds and baking powder. Add to the butter mixture and beat well. Fold in the clementine zest and juice and lemon juice before scraping the mixture into the prepared tin.

Bake in the oven for 50 minutes, or until a skewer inserted into the centre of the cake comes out clean.

To make the syrup, heat the honey with the clementine and lemon juice in a small pan over a gentle heat until runny, then pour over the cake whilst it's still hot. Leave to cool in the tin. Serve with Greek yoghurt or double cream.

## ≡ TIP ≡

You can experiment with other kinds of citrus in this recipe as well. It works very well with lemon. You can use agave nectar instead of honey for the syrup (this would go nicely with lime juice in place of the clementines).

# PINEAPPLE UPSIDE-DOWN CAKE

SERVES: 6

PREP TIME: 25 MINS + RESTING · COOK TIME: 45 MINS

V

125g **unsalted butter**, very soft

180g **caster sugar**

2 **free-range eggs**

1 teaspoon **vanilla extract**

1 teaspoon **salt**

100ml **whole milk**

210g **plain flour**

2 teaspoons **baking powder**

½ **pineapple**, skin and core removed, cut into rings (or tinned pineapple, if you like)

**CARAMEL:**

100g **unsalted butter**

150g **light brown sugar**

═ TIP ═

If the cake sticks, you can either pop it back in the oven to melt the caramel a little, or place the cake tin directly on the heat of the hob for a minute (no longer, or it could burn), which will melt the caramel and help release the cake.

*A carnival cake. Full of life. Full of flavour. A little bit kitsch. But deeply satisfying. You could substitute white spelt flour here very nicely.*

Heat the oven to 170°C/340°F/gas mark 3½.

First make the caramel. Put the butter and brown sugar in the bottom of a deep 20cm cake tin and place the tin directly over a gentle heat on the hob. Stir constantly until the butter-sugar mixture comes together and bubbles. Set aside to cool.

Cream the butter and caster sugar until light and fluffy. Add the eggs one at a time and mix until incorporated. Add the vanilla and salt. Add half the milk and mix.

Sift together the flour and baking powder and add half to the mixture. Add the remaining milk and finally the rest of the flour.

Now that the caramel in the tin has cooled, cover it with the pineapple rings. Over that, pour the cake batter and smooth the surface. Bake in the oven for about 40 minutes, until the top of the cake springs back when lightly pressed with a finger.

Let the cake sit in the tin for about 15 minutes before running a knife around the edge and inverting it on to a serving plate. If it is too hot, it can fall apart.

# TOMMI'S MORE-THAN-FRUIT CAKE

SERVES: 8

PREP TIME: 25 MINS + COOLING · COOK TIME: 55–60 MINS

V

375ml **red wine**

375g **dried figs**, chopped

1½ teaspoons **ground cinnamon**

¼ teaspoon **ground cloves**

125g **unsalted butter**, cold

250g **honey**, plus extra for drizzling

1 **free-range egg**, lightly beaten

200g **spelt flour**

1½ teaspoons **baking powder**

1 teaspoon **bicarbonate of soda**

**Greek yoghurt** or **soured cream**, to serve

*Red wine and figs have a special affinity for one another and the spices in this recipe. The fig seeds create a wonderful popping sensation as they burst in your mouth. Also a great way to use up leftover red wine.*

Heat the oven to 160°C/325°F/gas mark 3. Grease a 20cm square cake tin and line it with baking paper.

Put the red wine, figs and spices into a medium saucepan and bring to the boil.

When the fruit has plumped up a little (about 5 minutes), remove the saucepan from the heat and allow to cool for 10 minutes. Stir in the butter and honey and leave for another 10 minutes. Stir in the egg.

Sift the flour, baking power and soda into a large mixing bowl. Pour the fig mixture over the flour mixture and stir just until mixed. Pour into the prepared tin.

Bake for about 55–60 minutes, or until a skewer inserted into the centre of the cake comes out clean. Allow to cool in the tin. Serve with Greek yoghurt or soured cream, with extra honey for drizzling.

## ═ TIP ═

Can be served as a pud or at teatime.
A chunk in the lunchbox also makes
a great mid-morning snack.

# HANNAH'S BANANA BREAD

SERVES: 8–10

PREP TIME: 25 MINS + COOLING · COOK TIME: 55 MINS–1 HOUR

V

50g **pecan nut halves**

150ml **vegetable oil**, plus extra for greasing

200g **dark brown sugar**

1 teaspoon **vanilla extract**

2 **free-range eggs**

350g ripe **bananas**, peeled

75g **natural yoghurt**

1 teaspoon **bicarbonate of soda**

1 teaspoon **baking powder**

½ teaspoon **ground cinnamon**

¼ teaspoon **salt**

225g **wholemeal spelt flour**

**TOPPING:**

1 **banana**, peeled

3 tablespoons **caster sugar**

≡ TIP ≡

Never overmix the batter for quick breads like this, as they can easily go tough and rubbery.

*Some time ago people started leaving wishes on pieces of paper in a drawer in the Ludgate Circus branch of Leon. Hannah's wish was to have a cake named after her. Hence the name. This is a version of the classic bread made with spelt flour and a banana which sinks into the bread during cooking. It is the best banana bread we have tasted.*

Heat the oven to 170°C/340°F/gas mark 3½. Grease a 900g/2lb loaf tin and line it with baking paper. Line a baking tray with baking paper as well.

Spread the pecans out over the lined baking tray and toast them in the oven for about 5–7 minutes, or until lightly golden and fragrant. Set aside to cool.

In a large bowl, whisk together the oil, dark brown sugar, vanilla and eggs.

In a separate bowl, set aside a banana and roughly mash up the rest of them. Add the yoghurt and mix well. Sift the bicarbonate of soda, baking powder and cinnamon over the yoghurt mixture, add the salt and stir well to combine.

Now add the banana mixture to the egg mixture and stir to combine. Chop the pecans into small pieces and add them with the flour, stirring just until incorporated. Spoon the mixture into the prepared loaf tin.

Carefully slice the reserved banana in half lengthwise. Place one half, cut side up, on top of the bread and sprinkle with the caster sugar. (Eat the other half.)

Bake in the oven for 55–60 minutes, or until the bread is springy to the touch and a skewer inserted into the centre of the cake comes out clean. Cool in the tin for at least 10 minutes before turning it out on to a wire rack to cool.

# VANILLA CUPCAKES

MAKES: 12 CUPCAKES
PREP TIME: 15 MINS · COOK TIME: 25 MINS
WF · GF · DF · V · Ve

280g **self-raising gluten-free flour**

100g **potato flour** (or **cornflour** if you can't find potato)

70g **coconut flour** (fine desiccated coconut)

1 tablespoon **flax meal** (optional)

1½ teaspoons **sea salt**

150g **coconut oil**, melted

250ml **agave nectar**

2 tablespoons **vanilla extract**

150ml **rice milk**

½ teaspoon **bicarbonate of soda**

100ml boiling **water**

## ≡ TIPS ≡

The flax meal can be left out if you can't find it at your local health food shop, but it adds nutrition, texture and a nutty quality which we like.

The coconut oil can be replaced with a good-quality tasteless oil such as sunflower, but only if you really must. Coconut oil is full of nutrition.

These are delicious iced with the Vegan Vanilla Icing (overleaf).

*These cupcakes are free from wheat, refined sugar, dairy and egg. But, miraculously, full of flavour and indulgence. If you don't like the flavour of coconut, 1) you're crazy and 2) you can re-place the coconut flour with ground almonds.*

Heat the oven to 170°C/340°F/gas mark 3½, and line a 12-hole muffin tin with paper cases.

Put the gluten-free flour, potato flour, coconut flour, flax meal (if using) and sea salt into a large bowl. Use a balloon whisk or sieve to mix them together.

In another bowl, combine the melted coconut oil, agave nectar, vanilla extract and rice milk. In a small bowl, mix together the bicarbonate of soda and boiling water and then stir this into the other liquid ingredients.

Pour one third of the liquid ingredients into the dry and whisk together to make a batter, gradually adding the remaining liquid until all of it is incorporated.

Spoon the mixture into the paper cases and bake in the oven for 20–25 minutes, or until a skewer inserted in the centre of a cupcake comes out clean. These cakes are best eaten on the day they are made.

# VEGAN VANILLA ICING

MAKES: ENOUGH TO ICE 12 CUPCAKES
PREP TIME: 15 MINS + CHILLING
WF · GF · DF · V · Ve

350ml **unsweetened soya milk**, preferably Bonsoy

100g **almond milk powder** (not ground almonds)

50ml **agave nectar**

2 teaspoons **vanilla extract**

seeds from 1 **vanilla pod**

340g **coconut oil**, melted

2 tablespoons **fresh orange** or **clementine juice**

1 tablespoon **fresh lemon juice**

75g **cashew nut butter**

*We think this icing might be even better than the traditional butter and sugar version. It is the result of weeks spent by Claire testing different dairy- and allergen-free combinations. It is rich, but the coconut oil gives it a sublime melting consistency.*

With a stick blender or in a food processor, combine the soya milk, almond milk powder, agave and vanilla extract. Blend until smooth. Add the scraped seeds from the vanilla pod.

Combine the melted coconut oil with the orange and lemon juice and add to the mixture gradually, blending until smooth. Add the cashew nut butter and again blend until smooth.

Chill overnight before using so that the coconut oil solidifies. Remove from the fridge 30 minutes–1 hour before using, to soften.

## ═ TIPS ═

For pink icing, replace 150ml of the soya milk with 150ml of puréed and strained raspberries or strawberries. You can play with other natural colours and flavours, as with Royal Icing (see page 113).

If you can't do soya, substitute rice milk for the soya milk. The texture is not quite as smooth but the taste is great.

# BEN'S CLASSIC VICTORIA SPONGE

SERVES: 8
PREP TIME: 25 MINS + COOLING · COOK TIME: 40 MINS

330g **unsalted butter**, very soft,
plus extra for greasing

330g **caster sugar**, plus extra
for sprinkling

1 teaspoon **vanilla extract**

6 **free-range eggs**

330g **self-raising flour**

150g homemade or good-quality
bought **raspberry jam**

2 punnets of **fresh raspberries**
(if in season)

350ml **double cream**

*Classic recipes are classic because they have stood the test of time. This is the mother of all teatime cakes.*

Heat the oven to 160°C/325°F/gas mark 3. Grease two 25cm round cake tins and line them with baking paper.

In a large mixing bowl, beat together the soft butter and the sugar until very pale and fluffy. Add the vanilla extract and the eggs one at a time, alternating them with 1 tablespoon of flour and beating well after each addition. Once all the eggs have been added, add the remaining flour and mix well.

Divide the mixture between the 2 tins and bake in the oven for about 40 minutes, or until a skewer inserted in the centre of the cake comes out clean.

Cool the cakes for at least 10 minutes in the tins before turning out on to a wire rack to cool completely.

Just before serving, place one cake on a serving plate and slather it with the raspberry jam. Whip the cream to very soft peaks – just stiff enough to start to hold a shape – and layer that over the jam, reserving a good dollop for the top of the cake. Scatter the raspberries over the cream (saving 2 or 3 for decoration) and finish with the second cake layer. Sprinkle with caster sugar and put the last dollop of cream on top of the cake. Finish with the raspberries.

## ═ TIPS ═

This cake is best eaten right away, but it can be kept in the fridge in an airtight container for up to 3 days.

You can experiment with all sorts of different fruit fillings.

Try using thick yoghurt or soured cream instead of double cream.

# JOSSY'S LEMON PUDDING DELICIOUS

SERVES: 6

PREP TIME: 20 MINS · COOK TIME: 40 MINS

V

50g **unsalted butter**, at room temperature, plus extra for greasing

225g **golden caster sugar**

finely grated zest and juice of 2 large **lemons**

4 large **free-range eggs**, separated

50g **self-raising flour**

225ml **whole milk**

½ level teaspoon **cream of tartar**

**icing sugar**, for sprinkling (optional)

*This pudding was one that Henry's great granny Enid handed down to his mother, Jossy. It was cut out from a newspaper and was called 'Lemon Pudding' – next to it Enid had written 'delicious!'*

Heat the oven to 180°C/350°F/gas mark 4 and place a roasting tin half-filled with water on the centre shelf. Grease a 1.5–1.75 litre soufflé or other ovenproof dish.

Whisk the butter in a large bowl until soft, then add the sugar and whisk until fluffy. Gradually whisk in the lemon juice, followed by the lemon zest and the egg yolks.

Sift the flour on to the mixture and stir it in with a metal spoon, then gradually stir in the milk. Whisk thoroughly until very smooth.

In a clean bowl, whisk the egg whites with the cream of tartar using an electric hand mixer until they stand in soft peaks. Then, using a metal spoon, fold them gently into the pudding mixture, about one-quarter at a time.

Pour the mixture into the ovenproof dish and stand it in the roasting tin of water in the oven. Bake for 40 minutes, or slightly less in a fan oven, until risen and golden brown on top.

Serve hot or cold, with a little icing sugar sifted over the surface if you like.

# BETTER CARROT CAKE

SERVES: 8–10

PREP TIME: 30 MINS + COOLING · COOK TIME: ABOUT 1 HOUR

WF · GF · DF · V · Ve

250g **carrots**, peeled and grated

50g **apple** or **sweet potato**, peeled
and grated

50g **desiccated coconut**

50g **coconut oil**, melted

50ml **sunflower oil**, plus extra
for greasing

120ml **agave nectar**

1½ teaspoons **yacon syrup** (optional)

2 teaspoons **vanilla extract**

70g **gram flour** or **polenta flour**

140g **gluten-free plain flour**

1 teaspoon **xanthan gum**

1 teaspoon **bicarbonate of soda**

½ teaspoon **sea salt**

1½ teaspoons **ground cinnamon**

1 teaspoon **ground ginger**

180ml hot **water**

½ teaspoon **mandarin**, **lemon** or
**orange extract**

1 quantity **Vegan Vanilla Icing** (see
page 101)

*A beautiful carrot cake made without any dairy, wheat, gluten or refined sugar. Baking with the ingredients below takes some getting used to – the mixture will have a different consistency from a traditional wheat-based cake – but the results are worth the effort. Coconut oil and boiling water make the cake very moist. The rice flour gives the cake a fine texture and the spices and mandarin oil impart a unique flavour.*

Heat the oven to 160°C/325°F/gas mark 3. Grease a 900g/2lb loaf tin and line it with baking paper.

Combine the carrots, apple or sweet potato, coconut, coconut oil, sunflower oil, agave, yacon syrup and vanilla in a bowl and set aside.

Combine the dry ingredients in a second bowl and whisk together to evenly distribute them. Whisk in the carrot mixture.

Gradually pour in the hot water and citrus extract and mix to a smooth batter. Pour into the prepared tin.

Bake in the oven for 55–65 minutes, or until a skewer inserted into the centre of the cake comes out clean. Turn out of the loaf tin and allow to cool completely. Ice with vanilla icing.

## ═ TIP ═

As there is no gluten in this recipe, th
xanthan gum works as a binding agen
If you can't find it, you might find a se
raising gluten-free flour blend which
already contains it.

# TRIPLE CHOCOLATE FANTASY CAKE

SERVES: 12–15

PREP TIME: 25 MINS + COOLING · COOK TIME: 1 HOUR

V

200g **vegetable oil**, plus extra for greasing

400g **light brown sugar**

1½ teaspoons **vanilla extract**

3 **free-range eggs**

125ml **plain yoghurt**

80g **cocoa powder**

100ml boiling **water**

280g **plain flour**

1½ teaspoons **bicarbonate of soda**

½ teaspoon **salt**

**ICING:**

200g **unsalted butter**, softened

200g **icing sugar**

4–5 tablespoons boiling **water**

1 teaspoon **vanilla extract**

100g **cocoa powder**

**TO FINISH:**

4 tablespoons **apricot jam**

2 **Crunchie bars**, crumbled

**edible glitter** (can be found online and in speciality cake decorating shops)

*Honeycomb, chocolate and a hint of tangy apricot make this a dreamy treat. For extra decadence, add crumbled Crunchie bars between the layers.*

Preheat the oven to 160°C/325°F/gas mark 3. Grease 2 x 23cm cake tins and line them with baking paper.

Whisk together the oil, sugar and vanilla. Add the eggs one at a time, mixing well after each addition. Add the yoghurt and mix well.

In a small bowl, whisk together the cocoa powder and boiling water until smooth.

Scrape the cocoa paste into the egg mixture and combine into a smooth batter.

Sift together the flour, bicarbonate of soda and salt, and beat into the cake mixture just until incorporated.

Pour equal amounts into the cake tins and bake in the oven for 55–60 minutes or until a skewer inserted in the centre comes out clean. Leave to cool in the tins.

Now to make the icing. Beat the butter until fluffy, then gradually beat in the icing sugar. Add the boiling water and vanilla extract and beat for 3 minutes.

Add the cocoa powder and beat until fluffy.

To assemble, split each cake into 2 layers. Place the bottom layer on a serving plate and spread it with some of the apricot jam. Cover with a tablespoon of chocolate icing and follow with another layer of sponge. Repeat with the remaining layers, then ice the top and sides with the remaining icing. Decorate with crumbled Crunchie bars and edible glitter.

# COURGETTE BREAD

SERVES: 8–10

PREP TIME: 20 MINS + COOLING · COOK TIME: 50 MINS

V

200g **butter**, plus extra for greasing

200g **dark brown sugar**

3 **free-range eggs**

200g **courgettes**, washed and grated (skins left on)

200g **plain flour**

1 teaspoon **baking powder**

a pinch of **salt**

½ teaspoon **ground cinnamon**

*This sweet, dark bread is an American staple, but almost unknown in this country. They call it zucchini bread and eat it in the afternoon with a cup of coffee or tea. The cinnamon works very well with the courgette, and it's a great alternative to banana bread. Almost every ingredient in this recipe is weighed to 200g, which makes it pleasingly simple to learn by heart.*

Heat the oven to 170°C/340°F/gas mark 3½. Grease a 900g/2lb loaf tin and line it with baking paper.

Melt the butter in a small saucepan. Put the brown sugar into a large bowl and whisk in the eggs. Pour the melted butter into the bowl in a steady stream until well mixed in. Stir in the grated courgettes.

Put the plain flour, baking powder, salt and cinnamon into another bowl and stir them together.

Add the wet ingredients to the dry ingredients and mix just until incorporated. Pour into the prepared loaf tin and bake for 40–50 minutes, or until springy and a skewer inserted in the centre of the cake comes out clean. Allow to cool in the tin.

# ROYAL ICING

MAKES: ABOUT 800G, OR ENOUGH TO COVER A 20–25CM CAKE
PREP TIME: 10 MINS
WF · GF · DF · V

4 **free-range egg whites**
660g **icing sugar**
125ml **water** or **fruit purée**

*Swooped over a fruit cake or drizzled on cut-out cookies, royal icing is an old-fashioned edible decoration that – although incredibly sugary – is as classy as the name suggests. You don't need to reach for artificial colourings (although sometimes we think it's OK and sort of fun). Purée brightly coloured fruit to make natural colourings instead (see tip below), or try using powdered turmeric for a gorgeous yellow icing with a delicate aniseedy flavour.*

Put all the ingredients together in a bowl and use an electric mixer on a low speed to mix until combined. Then turn the speed up to medium for about 7 minutes, or until thick ribbons form.

You can make the icing softer or looser by adding a little more water.

## ≡ TIP ≡

Purée fruits that are fresh, ripe and vibrant-coloured by simply blending them to a pulp in a blender. Strain the purée to remove seeds and skin (except in the case of strawberries, which seem to benefit from keeping their little seeds in).

# PETRA'S FRUIT CAKE

**SERVES: 12–15**

**PREP TIME: 40 MINS + SOAKING AND COOLING · COOK TIME: 3½–4 HOURS**

**V**

225g **golden sultanas**

50ml **brandy**

225g good-quality **glacé cherries**, quartered

200g good-quality **candied peel**

125g **crystallized pineapple** or **papaya**, chopped

60g **crystallized ginger**, chopped into very small pieces

60g **candied angelica**, chopped into small pieces

125g **walnuts**, chopped

zest and juice of 1 **lemon**

225g **unsalted butter**, softened, plus extra for greasing

225g **caster sugar**

4 **free-range eggs**, at room temperature

225g **plain flour**

½ teaspoon **salt**

*This is another cake from the wonderful Petra (see page 84). This is the cake that she made for her daughters at their christenings, at their weddings and at the christenings of their own children. Word of its magnificence has spread, and with insane generosity Petra now seems to be in permanent production for friends and family. She varies the recipe a little each year, so as not to get bored. One of the nicest variations was the addition of 3 or 4 sugared apricots from Australia (not the ordinary dried ones). She cut down a little on the sugar and on the other fruit to compensate.*

Soak the sultanas in the brandy for several hours or overnight, then mix in the other fruits and the walnuts.

Prepare a deep 23–25cm cake tin – one with a loose bottom is best. Grease it and line it with 2 layers of baking paper. Round the outside of the tin, tie a band of paper that sticks up 2.5cm or so above the rim to give the cake extra protection.

Just before you are ready to start making the cake, add the lemon zest and juice to the fruit.

Heat the oven to 160°C/325°F/gas mark 3.

In a large bowl, cream the butter and sugar until pale and fluffy. In a separate bowl, beat the eggs really well with an electric hand whisk until foamy, thick and have increased in volume – this may take up to 10 minutes but it is worth it to get the right texture. Add the beaten eggs to the butter mixture a little at a time, beating well after each addition. (If the mixture shows any sign of curdling, beat in a tablespoon of the flour.) Stir in the remaining flour and then the salt.

Now you can stir in the prepared fruit and walnuts, a little at a time.

Turn the mixture into the prepared tin and smooth it over with the back of a spoon or a small metal spatula. Put the cake into the oven. After 1½ hours reduce the temperature to 140°C/275°F/gas mark 1 and bake for a further 2 hours. After the cake has been in the oven for at least 2 hours you can look to see if the top is browning too much. If it is, cover it with a double thickness of baking paper.

The cake is done when it is evenly risen and brown, and has shrunk from the sides of the tin.

Leave it in the tin to cool, away from draughts, for at least an hour before taking it out. Leave it to get quite cold before storing it in a large tin.

≡ TIPS ≡

The higher the quality of the crystallized fruit the better. Petra buys the whole crystallized ones from Harrods and chops them up herself (which might be going a bit far). Golden sultanas are essential, as they are so pretty. They can usually be found in Turkish shops.

Petra makes a christening cake by icing this Fruit Cake with Royal Icing (see page 113). Instead of aiming for smooth perfection, she ices this cake pretty roughly and then covers it with ribbons and a menagerie of little creatures bought from haberdashery shops.

PICTURED OVERLEAF ⟶

# WARM GOOEY CHOCOLATE CAKES

SERVES: 6–8
PREP TIME: 10 MINS · COOK TIME: 7 MINS
WF · GF · V

85g **unsalted butter**, plus extra
   or greasing
150g **dark chocolate**
a pinch of **salt**
5 tablespoons **cocoa powder**
100g **free-range egg whites** (about 2)
1 tablespoon **caster sugar**
**Chantilly cream**, to serve

*One of those chocolate-oozing-out-of-the-middle puddings that is not nearly as hard to make as your awestruck guests will assume.*

Heat the oven to 200°C/400°F/gas mark 6.

Grease 6 or 8 individual ramekins and sprinkle each one with some caster sugar.

Melt the butter, chocolate and salt in a large bowl over simmering water. When all is melted, sift in the cocoa powder.

In a separate bowl whisk together the egg whites and sugar until soft peaks form. Combine with the melted chocolate by folding gently and trying not to knock out too much air.

Spoon the mixture into the moulds and bake in the oven for just 7 minutes.

## ≡ TIP ≡

Whatever you do, do not over-bake these. They continue to bake slightly as they cool down, so take them out of the oven just before you think they are ready.

You can make the Chantilly cream by adding a small amount of sugar and vanilla extract to whipping cream.

This can also be served with pouring cream and a splash of Cognac if you have some around.

# A GOOD CHOCOLATE CAKE

SERVES: 8

PREP TIME: 30 MINS + COOLING · COOK TIME: 35 MINS

DF · V · Ve

150ml hot **water**

80g **cocoa powder**

200ml **agave syrup**

200ml **coconut milk**

juice of ½ **lemon**

80ml **sunflower oil**, plus extra for greasing

2 teaspoons **vanilla extract**

180g **white spelt flour** or **plain flour**

½ teaspoon **baking powder**

1½ teaspoons **bicarbonate of soda**

a pinch of **salt**

**flowers** from the garden, to decorate (optional)

**ICING:**

50g **coconut oil**

200g **dairy-free dark chocolate**

1 teaspoon **vanilla extract**

50ml **agave syrup**

*A great cake for a children's party if you don't want your house terrorized by children high on sugar and food colouring. It is vegan, but they'll never know it. It also looks ravishing decorated with flowers from the garden.*

Heat the oven to 160°C/325°F/gas mark 3. Grease and line a 20–23cm cake tin with baking paper.

Whisk together the hot water and cocoa powder until smooth. Add the remaining wet ingredients and set aside.

In a large bowl, sift together the flour, baking powder, bicarbonate of soda and salt. Pour the wet mixture over the dry and whisk in a circular motion from the centre of the bowl, moving outwards to combine. Pour the mixture into the cake tin.

Bake in the oven for about 35 minutes, or until a skewer inserted into the centre of the cake comes out clean and the cake is springy to the touch. Let the cake cool for 10 minutes before turning it out on to a wire rack to cool completely.

For the icing, put all the ingredients into a heatproof bowl and place over a pan of barely simmering water to melt, and stir. Move the cake to a serving plate and drizzle the chocolate icing over it. If you like, decorate with flowers from the garden.

## ≡ TIP ≡

Instead of flowers, you could add some raspberries to the cake and arrange a few on top for decoration.

# PETRA'S HONEY BREAD

. . . . . . . . . . . . . . . . . . . . . . . . . . . . . . . . . . . . . . . . . . . . . . . . . . . . . . . . . . . . . . . . .

**SERVES: 6–8**

**PREP TIME: 15 MINS + COOLING · COOK TIME: 1¼ HOURS**

**DF** (if oil is used for greasing and butter omitted) · **V**

. . . . . . . . . . . . . . . . . . . . . . . . . . . . . . . . . . . . . . . . . . . . . . . . . . . . . . . . . . . . . . . . .

**butter** or **oil**, for greasing

225g **plain flour**

115g **caster sugar**

115g **honey**, plus extra to glaze

150ml hot **water**

1 tsp **bicarbonate of soda**

zest of 1 **lemon**

*A sweet, soft, wonderfully moreish tea bread. Dangerously addictive with a thick topping of butter.*

. . . . . . . . . . . . . . . . . . . . . . . . . . . . . . . . . . . . . . .

Heat the oven to 160°C/325°F/gas mark 3. Grease a 450g/1lb loaf tin and line it with baking paper.

Mix together the flour and sugar in a large bowl.

In a small pan melt together the honey and the water.

Sprinkle the bicarbonate of soda over the water mixture and stir. Pour this over the dry ingredients, add the lemon zest and mix just until incorporated.

Turn the mixture into the prepared tin and bake in the oven for 1¼ hours.

Remove the bread from the tin and allow to cool, then brush with honey and serve thinly sliced.

## ═ TIP ═
Try replacing the lemon zest with orange or clementine zest.

# GUINNESS MALT CAKE

**SERVES: 8**
**PREP TIME: 15 MINS + COOLING · COOK TIME: 1½ HOURS**
**V** (if vegetarian stout is used)

250ml **Guinness** or other **stout beer**

250g **unsalted butter**, plus extra
for greasing

1 tablespoon **molasses** or **black treacle**

200g **dark brown sugar** or
**molasses sugar**

70g **cocoa powder**

2 tablespoons **powdered malt** (such as
Horlicks or Ovaltine)

2 **free-range eggs**

150g **plain yoghurt**

280g **plain flour**

2 teaspoons **bicarbonate of soda**

200g **caster sugar**

a pinch of **sea salt**

**STOUT AND CREAM CHEESE
FROSTING:**

100ml **Guinness** or other **stout beer**

60g **unsalted butter**, softened

120g **cream cheese**, softened

½ teaspoon **vanilla extract**

300g **icing sugar**, sifted

*A very moist and rich cake that marries the flavours of a good stout with malt and dark molasses. The dash of cocoa powder adds to the lovely colour. This cake will keep well for up to a week.*

Preheat the oven to 160°C/325°F/gas mark 3. Grease a 900g/2lb loaf tin and line it with baking paper.

Place the Guinness, butter, molasses and brown sugar in a small saucepan and melt over a medium heat. Whisk in the cocoa and malt, then take off the heat and allow to cool a little.

In a large bowl, whisk together the eggs and yoghurt, then add the stout mixture.

Sift together the remaining dry ingredients into the bowl and whisk together to combine. Pour into the prepared tin and bake in the oven for about 1¼ hours, or until a skewer inserted into the centre of the cake comes out clean. Cool the cake completely in the tin.

While the cake is cooling, make the icing: put the Guinness in a small pan and bring to the boil. Boil for about 10–15 minutes, or until the beer has reduced by half its volume. Pour into a container and pop it into the fridge to cool down.

In a mixing bowl, beat the soft butter until creamy and light. Add the cream cheese and beat until smooth. Add the vanilla and the sifted icing sugar and beat well. Now add the cooled, reduced Guinness and beat until creamy and light. Turn the cake out of its tin and spread the icing on top.

# LEON'S BIRTHDAY CAKE

SERVES: 12–15

PREP TIME: 40 MINS + COOLING AND CHILLING · COOK TIME: 50 MINS

V

125g **unsalted butter**, very soft, plus extra for greasing

200g **caster sugar**

3 **free-range eggs**

½ teaspoon **salt**

300g **self-raising flour**

175ml **coconut milk**

**SYRUP:**

150ml **coconut milk**

100g **sugar**

½ teaspoon **vanilla extract**

a pinch of **salt**

**FILLING:**

200ml **coconut milk**

100g **caster sugar**

80ml **water**

2 tablespoons **cornflour**, mixed with 4 tablespoons **water**

a pinch of **salt**

**TO DECORATE:**

300ml **whipped cream**

100g **coconut shavings**

*This cake looks crazy – like a gigantic, delicious powderpuff, or a Bounty bar turned inside out. It tastes amazing too. The coconut filling has the texture and flavour of very, very fresh coconut flesh.*

Heat the oven to 180°C/350°F/gas mark 4. Grease a 23cm cake tin and line with baking paper.

Cream the butter and sugar until almost white and fluffy. Add the eggs and salt and mix until fully incorporated. Add half the flour until just combined. Add the coconut milk and mix until combined. Then add the remaining flour and mix well.

Pour the mixture into the cake tin and smooth the top. Bake in the oven for 40–50 minutes, until a skewer inserted into the centre of the cake comes out clean and the cake springs back to the touch. Let the cake cool completely in the tin.

To make the filling, put the coconut milk, sugar and water into a heavy pan and place over a moderate heat. Stir to dissolve the sugar and then turn up the heat to high. Add the cornflour mixture to the pan with the salt and whisk until thick. Pour the mixture into a bowl and press clingfilm over the surface. Let it cool, then chill in the fridge for at least 2 hours.

To make the syrup, heat all the syrup ingredients together in a small saucepan and cook over a medium heat for 5 minutes.

Split the cooled cake into 3 layers. Drizzle with the syrup, and sandwich with the coconut filling. Cover the top and sides of the cake with whipped cream and sprinkle with generous amounts of coconut shavings.

# RUBY'S PEPPERMINT CREAM CUPCAKES

**MAKES: 12 CUPCAKES**

**PREP TIME: 30 MINS + COOLING · COOK TIME: 23 MINS**

**WF · GF · DF · V · Ve**

225g **gluten-free flour**

65g **cocoa powder**

1 tablespoon **baking powder**

1 teaspoon **fine sea salt**

115ml **sunflower oil**

190g **golden caster sugar**

1 teaspoon **vanilla extract**

2 teaspoons **peppermint oil**

140g **apple purée**

200ml hot **water**

**ICING:**

65g **vegan dairy-free spread**

325g **icing sugar**, sifted

½ teaspoon **vanilla extract**

1 teaspoon **peppermint oil**

a splash of **non-dairy milk** of choice
  (e.g. soya, oat, coconut, almond)

**TO DECORATE:**

**vegan chocolate**, melted, for drizzling

12 **fresh mint sprigs** (optional)

*Ruby started her vegan bakery with a stall in Greenwich Market, and now her cakes are a cult favourite across London. This particular one is John, our CEO's, favourite cake in the world. And he isn't even vegan.*

Preheat the oven to 170°C/340°F/gas mark 3½ and line a 12-hole muffin tin with cupcake cases.

In a large bowl, sift together the flour, cocoa, baking powder and salt.

In a separate bowl, mix together the oil, sugar, vanilla, peppermint oil and apple purée, until well combined. Add the hot water, then gradually add the dry ingredients to the wet, mixing between each addition until well combined.

Divide the mixture evenly between the 12 cupcake cases and bake in the oven for 23 minutes, until they have a shiny crust and a skewer inserted comes out clean. Allow to cool in the tin before decorating.

To make the icing, beat the vegan spread in a free-standing mixer or with an electric hand whisk, until smooth. Gradually add the icing sugar in small increments, beating as you go. Add the vanilla extract and peppermint oil, then gradually add small drops of milk, beating between each addition, until the icing is soft and smooth. Chill until the icing has firmed up a little.

Decorate the cupcakes with the icing, as desired. Top with a drizzle of melted chocolate and a fresh mint sprig if eating on the same day.

# TECHNICOLOR DREAM CAKE

SERVES: 10–12

PREP TIME: 25 MINS + COOLING · COOK TIME: 50 MINS

V

300g **plain flour**

½ teaspoon **salt**

4 teaspoons **baking powder**

200g **unsalted butter**, very soft, plus extra for greasing

400g **sugar**

1 teaspoon **vanilla extract**

4 **free-range eggs**, separated

225ml **milk**

**fresh fruit**, to decorate

**FOR EACH OF THE 4 LAYERS OF ICING:**

15ml **fresh fruit purée**, strained (we used raspberry, quince and strawberry), or a pinch of **turmeric**

30g **unsalted butter**, softened

150g **icing sugar**

**lemon juice** or **vanilla extract**

## ═ TIP ═

To make the icing, strain the fruit purée and set aside. In a medium bowl, beat the butter and sugar until light and fluffy. Add the fruit purée or turmeric, then taste. A little lemon juice or vanilla can balance the flavours of your icing nicely.

*A really fun cake to make, and lurid enough – despite the natural colours – to satisfy any child. The idea came from an old cake book Claire picked up at a charity shop.*

Heat the oven to 160°C/325°F/gas mark 3. Grease 2 x 23cm cake tins and line them with baking paper.

In a large bowl, sift together the flour, salt and baking powder and set aside.

Cream the butter and sugar until fluffy. Add the vanilla, then the egg yolks one at a time, mixing well after each addition. Add half the milk and mix well. Add half the flour mixture and combine. Repeat with the remaining milk and flour.

Whisk the egg whites in a clean bowl until soft peaks form. Stir one third of the egg whites into the cake mixture to lighten the batter and then fold in the remainder, taking care not to knock out too much air in the process.

Divide the mixture between the tins and bake in the oven for 45–50 minutes, or until a skewer inserted into the centre of the cake comes out clean. Leave the cakes to cool for 10 minutes before taking them out of the tins and letting them cool completely on a wire rack.

Split each layer in two and place the bottom of one on a cake stand. Slather with the first icing flavour, then continue to stack up the layers. Top with fresh fruit.

# BARS, BISCUITS & BUNS

# CUT-OUT BISCUITS

MAKES: 24 BISCUITS, DEPENDING ON SIZE
PREP TIME: 15 MINS + CHILLING AND COOLING · COOK TIME: 10–12 MINS
V

225g **unsalted butter**, very soft

400g **caster sugar**

2 **free-range eggs**

1 teaspoon **vanilla extract**

560g **plain flour**, plus extra for dusting

1 teaspoon **baking powder**

a pinch of **salt**

**Royal Icing** (see page 113)

*You need the right kind of dough to make cut-out biscuits – one that holds its shape during cooking. These biscuits should be a cornerstone of your baking repertoire, especially if you have young children – they're both tasty and a great way to keep the kids entertained.*

With an electric hand mixer, beat the softened butter with the caster sugar until light, pale and fluffy.

Add the eggs, one by one, then the vanilla extract.

Place the flour in a separate bowl and whisk in the baking powder and salt. Add half of this to the creamed mixture and beat on a low speed until just combined.

Add the remaining flour mixture and beat again to combine well.

Divide the dough in half and wrap each ball in clingfilm. You could freeze one ball for another time if you like. Chill for about 2 hours or overnight before using.

When ready to make the biscuits, heat the oven to 180°C/350°F/gas mark 4. Line a couple of baking trays with baking paper.

Lightly dust a surface with flour, then roll out the dough to about 5mm thick. Cut out shapes with your cutters and transfer the biscuits to your prepared baking trays. Chill for 15–20 minutes, then bake for 10–12 minutes or until just starting to turn golden. Transfer to a wire rack and leave to cool completely.

Decorate the biscuits with Royal Icing and leave out overnight to dry.

Store in an airtight container for up to a week.

## ═ TIP ═

Try adding flavours to the biscuits for variation. You can try the variations suggested on page 168, or add lemon zest, cinnamon or other spices you like. Henry is quite fond of ground cardamom seeds for a scented flavour.

# VIOLET COCONUT MACAROONS

**MAKES: 12 MACAROONS**
**PREP TIME: 15 MINS + COOLING · COOK TIME: 20 MINS**
**WF · GF · DF**

3 **free-range egg whites**
150g **caster sugar**
a pinch of **salt**
2 teaspoons **honey**
150g **desiccated coconut**
½ teaspoon **vanilla extract** (optional)

*There is a sublime crispy gooiness to these biscuits which makes them like nothing else on earth. Warning: they are very addictive. Violet is the name of Claire's bakery and shop on Wilton Way and her stall at Broadway Market, both in Hackney, London.*

Heat the oven to 150°C/300°F/gas mark 2. Line a baking tray with baking paper.

Combine the egg whites, caster sugar, salt, honey and desiccated coconut in a large pan over a medium heat.

Stir the mixture constantly until everything is dissolved and it just begins to scorch on the bottom. Take the pan off the heat and stir in the vanilla.

Let the mixture cool completely, then use an ice cream scoop (about 50ml) to scoop out 12 even-sized macaroons, and place them on the baking tray.

Bake in the oven for about 10–15 minutes, or until golden and set. Let the macaroons cool completely before peeling off the paper.

## ☰ TIP ☰

The key to getting these macaroons just right is to stir the ingredients in the pan until they begin to dry out.

# NANA GOY'S CRANBERRY FLAPJACKS

**MAKES: 16 FLAPJACKS**
**PREP TIME: 10 MINS + COOLING · COOK TIME: 30–35 MINS**
**WF · GF · V**

50g **dried cranberries**

55g **golden syrup**

170g **butter**, plus extra for greasing

100g **caster sugar**

250g **gluten-free rolled oats**

*These are moist and deliciously oaty like a good flapjack should be. We love them with dried cranberries but you could use any dried fruits (see tip below).*

Heat the oven to 180°C/350°F/gas mark 4, and grease a 20 x 20cm baking tin.

Put the cranberries into a bowl and cover with boiling water. Leave them for a few minutes until they are plump and rehydrated. Drain away the water and roughly chop any that are particularly large.

Melt the syrup, butter and sugar together in a large pan over a gentle heat until the sugar has dissolved, then stir in the oats. Add all but a small handful of the cranberries and stir thoroughly.

Tip the flapjack mixture into the tin and smooth it down with a spatula. Sprinkle the remaining cranberries on top. Bake in the oven for 30–35 minutes until golden. Mark into squares while still warm, and remove from the tin once cool.

## ≡ TIP ≡

For a fruity hit, try making them with chopped dates instead of cranberries. Add a handful of nuts and seeds to the mixture if you want to add another dimension to your flapjacks.

# ELISABETH'S LEMON BARS

MAKES: 8–10 BARS

PREP TIME: 30 MINS · COOK TIME: 45 MINS–1 HOUR

V

4 **free-range eggs**, beaten

350g **sugar**

120ml **fresh lemon juice** (Meyer or Amalfi if possible)

½ teaspoon grated **lemon zest** (Meyer or Amalfi if possible)

35g **plain flour**

1 teaspoon **baking powder**

**icing sugar**, to finish

**SHORTBREAD BASE:**

280g **plain flour**

80g **icing sugar**

1 teaspoon **salt**

225g **unsalted butter**, cold

*Sweet and gooey, with a sharp finish. An indulgent treat.*

Heat the oven to 170°C/340°F/gas mark 3½.

First make the shortbread base. Combine the flour, icing sugar, salt and cold butter in a food processor and mix until crumbly. If you don't have a food processor, cut the butter up with two knives, the back of a fork, or an old-fashioned pastry cutter.

Be careful not to let the butter get too warm either in the appliance or in your hands, as it changes the texture. Mix just until the dough forms a ball.

Press the dough into a 30 x 20cm baking tin.

Bake in the oven for 20–25 minutes or until golden and set, then leave to cool slightly while you get on with the topping.

Place the eggs in a bowl with the sugar, lemon juice and lemon zest. In a separate bowl, sift together the flour and the baking powder. Add to the egg mixture and stir to combine. Spread on to the cooled shortbread crust and return to the oven for 25–30 minutes, or until just set.

Cool completely in the tin. Sprinkle with icing sugar and cut into bars. These will keep well in an airtight container for up to 3 days.

= TIP =

Sprinkle with lavender flowers if you have them growing in your garden.

# CHERRY & ALMOND SLICE

MAKES: 14 SLICES
PREP TIME: 20 MINS + COOLING · COOK TIME: 25–30 MINS
WF · GF · V

200g **salted butter**, at room temperature

200g **golden caster sugar**

2 large **eggs**

¼ teaspoon **almond extract**

200g **fine polenta**

100g **ground almonds**

¼ teaspoon **gluten-free baking powder**

200g fresh **sour cherries**, pitted (frozen will also work)

30g **pistachios**, roughly chopped

4 teaspoons **milk**

4 teaspoons **lemon juice**

70g **icing sugar**

*This cake takes the title of 'most samples ever ordered to our Borough Market office before launch'. Which is to say, we may have ordered a few more samples than necessary because we couldn't stop snacking on it. This cake is made with whole sour cherries baked into a sponge with lemon juice and almond flour, making it taste like the lovechild of a lemon drizzle and a cherry bakewell. Perfect for the indecisive amongst us.*

Heat the oven to 180°C/350°F/gas mark 4 and line a 25 x 25cm deep baking tin with baking paper.

In a large bowl, beat together the butter and sugar until fluffy and smooth. Beat in the eggs, one at a time, then beat in the almond extract until well combined. Add the polenta, ground almonds and baking powder and fold in until well combined.

Scrape the mixture out into the lined tin and evenly sprinkle the sour cherries and pistachios over the surface of the batter, reserving about one-third of the pistachios for decorating.

Bake for 25–30 minutes, until just beginning to turn pale golden. Remove from the oven and let cool in the tin.

Meanwhile, combine the milk, lemon juice and icing sugar in a small saucepan and heat, whisking all the time, until the syrup is warm and no lumps of sugar remain.

Brush the hot syrup over the still-warm cake and sprinkle the reserved pistachios over the surface. Let the cake completely cool and set, then turn out of the tin and cut into slices or squares.

# SPELT HOT CROSS BUNS

· · · · · · · · · · · · · · · · · · · · · · · · · · · · · · · · · · · · · · · · · · · · · · · · · · · · · · · · · · · ·

**MAKES: 12 BUNS**
**PREP TIME: 50 MINS + RISING · COOK TIME: 15 MINS**
**DF · V · Ve** (if made with egg substitute)

· · · · · · · · · · · · · · · · · · · · · · · · · · · · · · · · · · · · · · · · · · · · · · · · · · · · · · · · · · · ·

2 x 7g sachets of **dried quick yeast**

200ml **rice milk**, warmed slightly, plus extra for brushing

200ml **agave nectar**

250g **strong wholemeal spelt flour**

250g **plain spelt flour**

1 teaspoon **salt**

½ teaspoon **ground allspice**

½ teaspoon freshly grated **nutmeg**

1 teaspoon **ground cinnamon**

75g **currants**

75g **sultanas**

zest of 1 **orange**

1 **free-range egg** or **egg substitute**

50g **coconut oil**, melted

**CROSSES:**

70g **strong spelt flour**

1 tablespoon **water**

**BUN WASH:**

75ml **water**

100ml **agave nectar**

*Wholesome and delicious. These buns are less sweet than most hot cross buns but just as festive. Toast them and slather with butter or coconut oil.*

· · · · · · · · · · · · · · · · · · · · · · · · · · · · · · · · · · · · · · · · · · · ·

Preheat the oven to 220°C/425°F/gas mark 7. Line 2 baking trays with baking paper.

Dissolve the yeast in the warm rice milk with the agave nectar and set aside.

In a separate bowl, combine the flours, salt, spices, currants, sultanas and zest.

Add the egg or egg substitute and the coconut oil to the milk mixture, then pour all of this over the dry ingredients. Stir the dough to combine and then cover and allow it to rest for about 20 minutes.

Turn the dough out on to a floured surface and knead it for 10–12 minutes, until it becomes silky. Put it back into the bowl and cover with a clean cloth. Leave in a warm place until the dough has nearly doubled in bulk. This should take about 3 hours.

Divide the dough into 12 pieces. Form each piece into a ball and place on the prepared baking trays, about 2cm apart. Allow the buns to rise on the trays for about 30–45 minutes, while you prepare the crosses.

Put the flour for the crosses into a small bowl and add water to make a paste. Brush the risen buns with a little rice milk. Use a piping bag with a small round nozzle (or make one out of paper), to pipe the paste in a cross over each bun. Bake in the oven for about 15 minutes, or until golden brown.

While the rolls are baking, make the bun wash by heating the water and agave nectar in a small pan. As soon as the buns come out of the oven, brush them with the wash. Serve warm or toasted.

# GOOD SCONES

**MAKES: 12 SCONES**
**PREP TIME: 20 MINS + RESTING AND COOLING · COOK TIME: 25 MINS**
**DF · V · Ve** (if cream substitute is used)

100g **gluten-free self-raising flour**

100g **white spelt flour**

2 teaspoons **gluten-free baking powder**

a large pinch of **salt**

50g **coconut oil**, melted, or **sunflower oil**

2 tablespoons **maple syrup**

1 tablespoon **vanilla extract**

80ml hot **water**

50ml **rice milk**

**clotted cream** or **cream substitute** and **strawberry jam**, to serve

*These scones are made with lots of alternative ingredients that make them healthier. But we like the idea of eating them with clotted cream and strawberry jam anyway.*

Measure all the dry ingredients into a large bowl. In a small saucepan, melt the coconut oil and let it cool slightly. Pour the oil over the dry ingredients and toss together with a fork.

Mix the remaining ingredients, except the cream and jam, into the dry ingredients just until combined. Don't overwork it.

Let the dough rest for 10 minutes. Meanwhile, line a baking tray with baking paper, and heat the oven to 180°C/350°F/gas mark 4.

Roll out the dough to 1.5–2cm thick. Use a biscuit cutter or a glass to cut out about 12 round discs.

Place the scones on the baking tray and bake in the oven for 20–25 minutes.

When they are ready and firm to the touch, take them out of the oven and place on a cooling rack. Cool completely before splitting open and filling with cream and jam.

## ═ TIP ═

You could make the scones wheat- and gluten- free by omitting the spelt flour and using either more of the gluten-free self-raising flour or substituting gram flour for the spelt.

# ECCLES CAKES

**MAKES: 12 CAKES**

**PREP TIME: 15 MINS + CHILLING · COOK TIME: 25 MINS**

V

125g **unsalted butter**

320g **dark brown sugar**

450g **currants**

2 teaspoons **ground cinnamon**

½ teaspoon **nutmeg**, freshly grated

zest of 1 **orange**

1 x 375g packet of **puff pastry**

**plain flour**, for dusting

1 **free-range egg** or **egg yolk**, for glazing

1 tablespoon **single cream**

*These Lancashire currant cakes are a quintessentially English treat, and are amazing served with a crumbly, mild Lancashire cheese. But only eat one: they are so rich that they were banned by the Puritans lest they agitate ungodly humours.*

Melt the butter with the sugar, currants, cinnamon, nutmeg and orange zest.

Chill for at least 1 hour, then divide the mixture into 12 balls. Heat the oven to 180°C/350°F/gas mark 4 and line a baking tray with baking paper.

Roll out the pastry on a floured surface and cut into 12 squares, 10cm across. Place a ball of filling on each one, then bring the edges together around the ball of filling and pinch to seal so the filling does not escape when cooking.

Place, seam side down, on the baking tray and chill for 10 minutes.

In a small bowl, mix the egg or egg yolk and cream together with a fork, to make an egg wash. Brush the cakes with the egg wash, then use scissors to snip 3 small holes in the top of each cake. Bake in the oven for about 20–25 minutes until golden and risen. Transfer to a wire rack to cool.

## ═ TIP ═

Try adding a drop of rum to the currant mixture – a trick apparently used to help preserve them when the Lancastrians exported them in the early 19th century.

# MAGGIE'S BEST CHOCOLATE CHIP COOKIES

**MAKES: 24 COOKIES**
**PREP TIME: 15 MINS · COOK TIME: 11 MINS**
**WF · GF · V**

280g **gluten-free plain flour**
2 teaspoons **gluten-free baking powder**
½ teaspoon **sea salt**
200g **dark chocolate chips** or **chunks**
50ml **agave nectar**
200ml **maple syrup**
125g **unsalted butter**, melted
1 tablespoon **vanilla extract**
**sea salt**, for sprinkling (optional)

*Gooey, chocolatey, but without the wheat flour or refined sugar.*

Heat the oven to 180°C/350°F/gas mark 4. Line a baking tray with baking paper.

Mix together all the dry ingredients in a medium bowl (including the chocolate chips or chunks).

Mix together all the wet ingredients in a small bowl.

Add the wet ingredients to the dry ingredients, and stir until they are well combined, but do not overmix.

Drop spoonfuls of the cookie dough on to the prepared baking tray. Lightly sprinkle with sea salt if desired.

Bake in the oven for only 11 minutes, and allow the biscuits to cool on the tray for 1 minute before transferring to a cooling rack.

## ═ TIPS ═

Following the baking time instructions will give you the perfect gooey texture.

If you can't get hold of gluten-free flour and you don't mind the gluten, normal flour can be substituted.

# BAR OF GOOD THINGS

. . . . . . . . . . . . . . . . . . . . . . . . . . . . . . . . . . . . . . . . . . . . . .

**MAKES: 8 BARS**
**PREP TIME: 20 MINS + SOAKING · COOK TIME: 2 HOURS**
**WF · GF · DF · V · Ve**

. . . . . . . . . . . . . . . . . . . . . . . . . . . . . . . . . . . . . . . . . . . . . .

175g **sesame seeds**, preferably soaked
    and dried

110g **cashew nuts**, finely chopped

a pinch of **sea salt**

2 tablespoons **brown rice syrup**

2 tablespoons **tahini**

2 tablespoons **yacon syrup**

2 teaspoons **lemon zest**

60g **roasted, salted pistachios**, shelled
    and roughly chopped

80g **dried apricots**, chopped

**FIG PASTE:**

60ml **water**

1 teaspoon **vanilla extract**

80g **dried figs**

1¼ teaspoons **ground ginger**

¼ teaspoon **ground cumin**

**COATING:**

80g **sesame seeds**, lightly toasted

*Well, you are what you eat.*

. . . . . . . . . . . . . . . . . . . . . . . . . . . . . . . . . .

Heat the oven to 110°C/225°F/gas mark ½. Line a 30 x 20cm baking tin with baking paper.

For the fig paste, heat the water with the vanilla in a small pan and pour over the dried figs. Allow to soak for 15 minutes, then blend with the ginger and cumin to form a paste.

Meanwhile, mix the sesame seeds, cashews and salt in a medium bowl.

Mix the brown rice syrup, tahini, yacon and lemon zest in a small bowl and stir in the fig paste.

Add the wet ingredients to the dry ingredients and mix well (this is easiest done with your hands, as the mixture should be quite stiff). Then fold in the pistachios and apricots.

Sprinkle half the sesame seeds for coating into the prepared baking tin, then press the mixture evenly on top so it is 1–1.5cm thick. Sprinkle over the remaining seeds.

Bake in the oven for 1 hour, then flip it over, put it back in the tin and bake for 1 more hour. Allow to cool in the tin. Cut into bars and keep in an airtight container.

## ≡ TIP ≡

The yacon syrup can be replaced by more brown rice syrup or agave nectar.

# BETTER BROWNIE

**MAKES: 12 LARGE BROWNIES**
**PREP TIME: 25 MINS · COOK TIME: 35 MINS**
**WF · GF · V**

180g **unsalted butter**, plus extra
    for greasing

200g **dark chocolate** (54% cocoa solids)

1 **orange**

2 teaspoons **espresso** or **strong coffee**

80g **whole almonds** (skins on)

4 **free-range eggs**

100g **ground almonds**

160g **dark chocolate chunks** (54%
    cocoa solids)

160g **very dark chocolate chunks** (70%
    cocoa solids)

150g **brown sugar**

a pinch of **sea salt**

3–4 drops of **vanilla extract**

*We have been selling these brownies at LEON since we opened our first restaurant in London's Carnaby Street in 2004. They were developed by Emma Goss-Custard, one of our favourite bakers. Her stroke of genius was to add some very strong espresso and orange zest, with their bitter and citrus notes contrasting perfectly against the sweet chocolate chunks.*

Heat the oven to 180°C/350°F/gas mark 4. Generously grease a 30 x 20 x 5cm baking tray, or one of similar dimensions.

Melt the butter in a small pan, and allow it to cool slightly.

In a separate bowl, melt the dark chocolate in a heatproof bowl set over a pan of hot water, stirring well to make sure that it is properly melted, and being careful not to burn it. Finely grate the orange zest directly into the melted chocolate to catch the oils that are released during the zesting process.

Add the coffee to the melted butter.

On another baking tray, spread out the whole almonds and toast in the oven for 10 minutes, then roughly chop.

Crack the eggs into a large mixing bowl. Add the ground almonds, the chopped almonds, all the chocolate chunks and the sugar. Stir in the salt and vanilla, followed by the melted chocolate and butter mixture.

Mix well until creamy and thickened, but do not overmix, as too much air will cause the brownie to crumble when baked.

Spoon the mixture into the prepared baking tray and place in the oven for approximately 20–25 minutes. Take great care not to over-bake the brownies. They are ready when the edges are slightly crusty but the middle is still soft.

Remove from the oven and allow to cool in the tin.

═ TIP ═

You can replace the brown sugar with 150g of fructose. Fructose turns a much darker colour when baked than sugar. The brownie develops a glossy sheen and will not look cooked, when in fact it is. Resist the temptation to cook it for too long.

PICTURED OVERLEAF ➞

# LISE'S CHERRY ALMOND COOKIES

**MAKES: 15–20 COOKIES**
**PREP TIME: 20 MINS · COOK TIME: 10–12 MINS**
**V**

200g **salted butter**, softened, plus extra
for greasing

235g **soft brown sugar**

2 small **free-range eggs**

130g **plain flour**

½ teaspoon **bicarbonate of soda**

185g **rolled oats**

150g **dried sour cherries**

50g **flaked almonds**

75g **chocolate chips**

*The recipe below is based on Lise's oat and raisin cookies, but with a sweet summer twist to it. If you want to make a version of the original, just replace the chocolate chips, cherries and almonds with raisins.*

Heat the oven to 180°C/350°F/gas mark 4. Grease several large baking trays or line them with baking paper.

Cream together the butter and the sugar, then add the eggs, one at a time, and beat until light and fluffy.

In another bowl, combine the flour, bicarbonate of soda, oats, cherries, flaked almonds and chocolate chips. Add to the butter mixture, taking care not to overmix the dough.

Use an ice cream scoop or 2 tablespoons to scoop 5cm balls of dough (about 50g each) on to the baking trays. Space the balls about 12cm apart. Each cookie will spread to about 10cm. If your dough is cold, the cookies will not spread as well, in which case you will need to flatten them a little with the palm of your hand before baking.

Bake in the oven for 10–12 minutes, or until golden (you may need to bake them in batches). The cookies will be very soft when you take them out, but will become firmer as they cool down. Leave them on the baking trays for a few minutes before transferring them to a wire rack to cool completely. Store in an airtight container.

# LEMON, COURGETTE & POLENTA TRAYBAKE

**MAKES: 16 SLICES**
**PREP TIME: 20 MINS · COOK TIME: 25–30 MINS**
**WF · GF · DF · V**

200g **golden caster sugar**

zest of 2 **lemons**

2 large **free-range eggs**

200g **rapeseed oil**

120g **fine polenta**

100g **ground almonds**

1 teaspoon **gluten-free baking powder**

¼ teaspoon **salt**

150g **courgette**, grated

20g shelled **pistachios**, finely chopped

**dried rose petals**, for sprinkling

**LEMON SYRUP:**

50ml **lemon juice**

50g **golden caster sugar**

*The first disclaimer we need to make about this cake is: no, you can't taste the courgette. The second is: it's really, really good. The polenta base soaks up all of the lemon syrup making it extra (sorry) moist, and the rose petals and pistachios scattered on top give it a fragrant, nutty finish. A recipe from our friend, Mike Smart.*

Heat the oven to 180°C/350°F/gas mark 4 and line a 25 x 25cm deep baking tin with baking paper.

In a large bowl, beat together the sugar and lemon zest, until the sugar is the consistency of damp sand. Add the eggs and oil to the mixture and beat until smooth and well combined. Add the polenta, ground almonds, baking powder and salt and fold in until well combined, then fold in the courgette.

Scrape the batter into the lined tin and bake for 25–30 minutes, until just beginning to turn pale golden.

Meanwhile, make the syrup. In a small saucepan, heat the lemon juice and caster sugar, stirring until the sugar has completely dissolved and a warm syrup has formed.

Evenly sprinkle the chopped pistachios and dried rose petals over the surface of the still-warm cake, then use a spoon to drizzle over the warm lemon syrup.

Let the cake cool completely, then turn out of the tin and cut into slices or squares.

≡ TIP ≡

You could experiment with the flavours in this recipe by substituting the lemon zest and juice with equal quantities of another citrus fruit, such as orange or grapefruit.

PICTURED OVERLEAF ⟶

# OAT & CRANBERRY COOKIES

MAKES: 24 COOKIES

PREP TIME: 20 MINS, PLUS RESTING (OPTIONAL) · COOK TIME: 20–23 MINS

V

150g **light brown sugar**

75g **caster sugar**

225g **unsalted butter**

200g **plain flour**

½ teaspoon **ground cinnamon**

1 teaspoon **baking powder**

1 teaspoon **fine sea salt**

2 **eggs**

125g **jumbo rolled oats**

50g **sultanas**

50g **dried cranberries**

50g **hazelnuts**

50g shelled **pistachios**

*The perfect ratio of crispy edges to gooey centre.*

Heat the oven to 160°C/325°F/gas mark 3 and line 2 baking trays with baking paper.

In a large bowl, combine the sugars and butter and beat until fluffy.

In a separate bowl, sift together the flour, cinnamon, baking powder and ½ teaspoon of the salt, then tip into the butter mixture and mix to combine. Add the eggs, one at a time, mixing thoroughly after each addition, until you have a dough that is sticky and soft.

In the same bowl that held the flour, combine the oats, dried fruits and nuts with the remaining ½ teaspoon of salt, then add to the dough mixture and give it one final mix to combine. If you have time, transfer the dough to the fridge to rest for 1 hour (this will help prevent the cookies from spreading too much in the oven).

Scoop heaped tablespoons of the dough mixture onto the prepared baking trays, making sure they are well spaced to allow for spreading. Bake for 20–23 minutes, until golden. Let the cookies cool on the trays for 2–3 minutes, before transferring to a wire rack to cool completely.

# ALMOND, DATE & OAT MUFFINS

**MAKES: 12 MUFFINS**
**PREP TIME: 20 MINS · COOK TIME: 25 MINS**
**V**

100g **whole almonds** (skins on)

200g **unsalted butter**, melted

75g **light brown sugar**

200g **oat bran**

100g **rolled oats**, plus extra for sprinkling

200g **fine spelt flour**

½ teaspoon **salt**

1½ teaspoons **bicarbonate of soda**

2 **free-range eggs**

350ml **plain yoghurt**

250g pitted chopped **dates**

zest of 1 **orange**

*A nutty, semi-sweet breakfast muffin made with spelt flour, which is not only better for you than other varieties of wheat, but gives it its distinctive texture and flavour.*

Heat the oven to 170°C/340°F/gas mark 3½. Grease a 12-hole muffin tin or line it with paper cases.

Spread the almonds out on a baking tray and toast in the oven for 5–7 minutes, or until golden.

Melt the butter and sugar in a small saucepan and set aside to cool slightly.

In a large bowl, mix together the oat bran, rolled oats, spelt flour, salt and bicarbonate of soda. Roughly chop the toasted almonds and stir them into the dry ingredients.

In a separate bowl, whisk together the eggs and yoghurt and stir in the dates and orange zest. Whisk in the melted butter and sugar and pour all of the wet mixture over the dry ingredients. Mix just until combined.

Spoon the mixture into the muffin tin and bake in the oven for 20–25 minutes, until the muffins are golden.

≡ TIP ≡
You could also make these muffins with dates that have been soaked in juice or alcohol.

# HALLOWEEN BISCUITS

PREP TIME: 30 MINS + MAKING THE BISCUITS

V

1 quantity **Cut-out Biscuits** (see page 135)
**writing icing tubes**, for drawing
**sprinkles**, to decorate

**FOR EACH COLOUR ICING:**
1 tablespoon **water**
a few drops of **food colouring**
**icing sugar**

*Make the Cut-out Biscuits on page 135, adding either ½ teaspoon of mixed spice to make some autumnal lightly spiced biscuits, or substitute 60g cocoa powder for 60g flour to make them chocolatey.*

Make a few coloured icings in different bowls by mixing the water and food colouring, then adding icing sugar until the icing is thick and smooth (not too runny).

Using the icings as backgrounds and the writing icing tubes for the detail, unleash the creative beast in you. If you're making these with children, you really ought to let them do the decorating. Lay out lots of little bowls filled with sugary things to stick on to the icing – hundreds and thousands, silver sugar balls, Smarties, whatever – and let them go mental.

# DESSERTS

# PAVLOVA

SERVES: 6

PREP TIME: 20 MINS + COOLING · COOK TIME: 2 HOURS

WF · GF · V

3 **free-range egg whites**

¼ teaspoon **salt**

½ teaspoon **white wine vinegar**

½ teaspoon **vanilla extract**

300g **caster sugar**

1½ teaspoons **cornflour**


**TO SERVE:**

3 tablespoons **raspberry jam**

200ml **double cream**, lightly whipped

600g **strawberries**

2 tablespoons **caster sugar**

3 **passion fruit**

*There are hundreds of ways to dress a pavlova, but this is our favourite: simple and clean and drizzled with the sharp, juicy pulp of passion fruit. We like to serve it up on individual meringues, to make the recipients feel extra special.*

Heat the oven to 120°C/250°F/gas mark ½. Line a baking tray with baking paper.

Using an electric hand mixer, beat the egg whites, salt, vinegar and vanilla on a high speed until soft peaks form.

Whisk 200g of the sugar and the cornflour together by hand and add half to the frothy egg whites. Use the electric hand whisk to whip until very stiff, then add the remaining half. Whisk until stiff again, then add the remaining 100g of sugar. Whisk until smooth and glossy.

Spoon 6 large swoops of the meringue on to your baking tray, 4cm apart.

Bake in the oven for about 2 hours, then check the meringues. Remove from the oven when dry and firm. It should be possible to peel them gently off the paper. If they stick to the paper they're not ready. Cool completely when cooked.

To assemble, place the meringues on a large serving plate or individual plates. Put a spoonful of raspberry jam on each and then a generous dollop of cream.

Quarter the strawberries and toss with the caster sugar. Leave to macerate for a few minutes while you halve the passion fruits. To save time, you can prepare the strawberries up to 2 hours in advance and keep them in the fridge.

Stir the strawberries and divide between the pavlovas. Scoop out half a passion fruit on to each and serve.

## ≡ TIPS ≡

Making meringue can be intimidating, but it needn't be when you know a few tricks and you have the right tools. An electric hand whisk or free-standing mixer is always going to make meringue-making easier. Meringue can take an incredible amount of beating (unlike cream) so it is hard to overdo it. The salt and cornflour help to stabilize the whites and keep them from 'breaking'.

Meringues can be made up to 5 days in advance and kept in an airtight container.

The trick to making successful meringues is to open the oven door a few times during the baking to let condensation out. The idea is to dry out the exterior of the meringues while keeping the inside moist.

PICTURED OVERLEAF ⟶

# BLUEBERRY CHEESECAKE

SERVES: 8–10
PREP TIME: 20 MINS + CHILLING AND COOLING · COOK TIME: 45 MINS–1 HOUR
V

125g **digestive biscuits**
125g **gingernut biscuits**
90g **unsalted butter**
550g **cream cheese**
125g **caster sugar**
2 teaspoons **lemon juice**
seeds from 1 **vanilla pod**
200g **crème fraîche** or **soured cream**
100g thick **Greek yoghurt**
3 large **free-range eggs**

**BLUEBERRY TOPPING:**
2 small punnets of **blueberries**
2 teaspoons **cornflour**
3 tablespoons **water**

*A rich, creamy cheesecake cut by a sharper fruit topping. Luxurious.*

Heat the oven to 160°C/325°F/gas mark 3.

Crush the biscuits to a fine powder in a food processor. Decant them into a bowl. Melt the butter and pour it over the biscuit crumbs, stirring to fully coat them.

Press the biscuit mixture into the base of a deep 20cm springform or loose-bottomed cake tin, then put it into the fridge to firm up.

Beat the cream cheese, caster sugar, lemon juice and seeds scraped from the vanilla pod together until creamy. Mix in the crème fraîche and yoghurt, then the eggs and beat until smooth.

Spoon the filling over the chilled biscuit base. Smooth over the top and bake in the oven for 45 minutes, or until the filling has set (it may need a further 10 minutes).

Place the tin on a wire rack to cool completely, then run a small paring knife around the inside of the tin to help release the cheesecake and transfer to a serving plate.

Toss the blueberries in the cornflour and put them in a small saucepan with the water. Heat whilst stirring until the blueberries are bubbling and start to break up. Allow to cool then spoon over the top of the cheesecake.

## ≡ TIP ≡
Cherries are always welcome on a cheesecake, as are cranberries. Add a teaspoon of almond extract to the cheesecake mixture for the cherry version, and finely grated orange zest for the cranberry version.

# BAKED APPLES

**SERVES: 4**

**PREP TIME: 15 MINS · COOK TIME: 30–45 MINS**

**DF · V · Ve** (**WF · GF** if gluten-free bread is used and mincemeat is checked)

4 medium **apples**, such as Cox's
or Braeburn

1 slice of stale **bread**, white or gluten-free

150g homemade or other good-quality
vegan **mincemeat**

a pinch of **sea salt**

**custard** or **double cream**, to serve
(optional)

*Baked apples are easy and perfect for a chilly autumn night. They deserve to be more fashionable than they are.*

Heat the oven to 180°C /350°F/gas mark 4. Line a baking tray with baking paper.

Dig out the cores of the apples without going all the way through to the bottom, then place them on individual squares of kitchen foil, big enough to wrap the apples, on the lined baking tray.

Tear the bread into pea-sized pieces and mix with the mincemeat and salt. Pack the bread mixture into the apples. Bring the foil up and wrap it loosely around them, then bake in the oven for 30–45 minutes, until tender.

Serve with custard or double cream, if you like.

## ALTERNATIVE TOPPINGS

Instead of mincemeat, the following
work well as toppings:

• Raspberries, brown sugar and
breadcrumbs, served with vanilla
ice cream.

• Dried apricots, sultanas and dried sour
cherries, plumped in red wine and sugar,
drizzled with butter and served with
double cream.

# JOSSY'S JEWELLED RHUBARB & MANGO

SERVES: 4

PREP TIME: 20 MINS · COOK TIME: 1 HOUR

WF · GF · DF · V · Ve

500g early forced thin-stalked **champagne rhubarb**

1.5cm piece of **fresh ginger**

2 or 3 **star anise**

150ml **cranberry juice**

juice of 2 **limes**

50g **caster sugar**

1 large or 2 small ripe **mangoes**

a few **mint leaves**, to decorate

*This is a simple but sublime combination, which also looks beautiful. The appearance of the deep yellow mango with the clear pink rhubarb, and the combination of their contrasting flavours, is wonderful.*

Heat the oven to 170°C/340°F/gas mark 3½.

Slice the rhubarb across on the diagonal into 5cm pieces. Peel the ginger and cut into very thin mathsticks.

Arrange the rhubarb, ginger and star anise in a wide ovenproof dish. Put the cranberry juice, lime juice and sugar into a saucepan and bring to the boil, stirring until the sugar has dissolved. Boil fiercely for 2 minutes, then pour on to the rhubarb.

Cover the dish tightly with foil and put it on the centre shelf of the oven for about 1 hour, until the rhubarb is very soft. Remove the foil and leave to cool completely.

Cut the mango flesh off the stone, then peel them and slice into thin strips. Arrange the mango strips among the rhubarb, with the star anise dotted on top, then chill in the fridge. Decorate with mint leaves before serving.

# BAKED ALASKA

500g **vanilla** or **strawberry ice cream**
(or any favourite flavour)

1 x 20cm round **sponge cake** (store-
bought, or made using ¼ quantity
of **Ben's Classic Victoria Sponge**,
see page 102)

4 **free-range egg whites**, at room
temperature

¼ teaspoon **cream of tartar**

200g **caster sugar**

*This is fun to make, easier than you would think, and will make your guests squeal with nostalgic delight.*

Line a 20cm-diameter bowl with clingfilm.

Take the ice cream of your choice and allow to soften slightly out of the freezer. Pack the ice cream into the bowl very tightly to make a neat dome shape and cover with more clingfilm. Place in the freezer for at least 3 hours.

Heat the oven to 220°C/425°F/gas mark 7. Place the sponge cake on a baking tray lined with baking paper and set aside.

Put the egg whites into a large clean bowl, and use an electric hand mixer to whisk them into soft peaks. Add the cream of tartar, then gradually add the sugar. Whisk until super stiff and glossy.

Take the ice cream out of the freezer and discard the top layer of clingfilm. Dunk the bottom of the bowl into a sink of hot water for a second. Invert the bowl over the sponge and use the clingfilm to help coax the ice cream from the bowl. Discard the clingfilm and immediately cover the ice cream with the meringue. Use a knife to coax the meringue into peaks.

Bake in the oven for 5 minutes, until the peaks are golden.

Serve immediately!

## ═ TIP ═

To ensure the meringue does not slide off the sides of the ice cream as you assemble it, we find that the real trick is to have very stiff meringue and very cold ice cream.

# CRÈME BRÛLÉE

**SERVES: 4**
**PREP TIME: 20 MINS · COOK TIME: 30–40 MINS**
**WF · GF · V**

590ml **double cream**

1 **vanilla pod**

6 **free-range egg yolks**

50g **caster sugar**, plus 4 tablespoons

*Henry maintains that you can gauge the quality of any restaurant by one mouthful of its crème brûlée. Yet it's not particularly hard to make well, and is terrifically impressive when you do. This – together with its swoonsome creaminess – makes it a perfect Valentine's Day pudding, especially with the addition of heart-shaped ramekins.*

Heat the oven to 150°C/300°F/gas mark 2. Have ready 4 heart-shaped or standard ramekins.

Pour the cream into a pan. Cut the vanilla pod in half lengthwise and scrape the seeds into the cream, also adding the empty pod.

Heat to just below boiling point, then remove from the heat and allow the vanilla to infuse for 10 minutes before discarding the empty pod.

Meanwhile, whisk the egg yolks together with the 50g of sugar until the mixture is pale and thick. Add the infused cream. Stir well before pouring into the 4 ramekins.

Place the ramekins in a deep roasting tin. Fill the tin with water to come about halfway up the sides of the ramekins, then cover the tin tightly with foil and bake in the oven for 30–40 minutes, or until the custard is set but still wobbly. Remove from the oven and allow the custards to cool without the foil covering. Chill in the fridge until ready to serve.

To make the brûléed top, sprinkle a tablespoon of sugar over each pudding (do them one at a time) and, using a blowtorch or a very hot grill, heat the sugar until burnt. Let the burnt sugar shell set for 5 minutes before serving.

We are opposed to the fashionable habit of adding berries to crème brûlée. It interferes with the pure creaminess of the dish. However, if you must make variations, there are a few interesting flavours that work well:

- Indian: use 4 crushed cardamom pods instead of the vanilla.

- Boozy: add a tot of rum or brandy to the custard.

- Orange: steep a couple of teaspoons of finely grated orange zest in the cream, with or without the vanilla pod.

- Thanksgiving: add a little pumpkin purée and nutmeg. It works. Not on Valentine's Day, please.

## ═ TIP ═

This dessert is perfect for making in advance. The custard can be made the day before and chilled in a jug overnight. You can bake the custard in the morning, then pull the ramekins out of the fridge at the end of supper, brûlée them and send them straight to the table.

**PICTURED OVERLEAF ⟶**

# ROASTED QUINCE COMPOTE

SERVES 6–8

PREP TIME: 15 MINS · COOK TIME: APPROX. 1¾ HOURS

WF · GF · DF · V · Ve

3 **quinces**

1 **bay leaf**

1 large strip of **lemon peel**

½ a **vanilla pod**, split in half lengthwise

250ml **water**

250g **granulated sugar**

*Lovely with cheese after dinner, and an awful lot easier than making membrillo (a traditional Spanish quince paste boiled for hours). The compote also goes well with panna cotta and other creamy puddings, or on top of a good yoghurt for breakfast.*

Heat the oven to 200°C/400°F/gas mark 6.

Peel and quarter the quinces (don't worry about coring them until after they have been baked, when they are soft and easier to manage). Arrange them in a roasting tin large enough that they have a little room around them.

Add the bay leaf, lemon peel and vanilla pod and cover with the water and sugar. Cover tightly with foil and bake for 1 hour.

Remove the foil, then turn the heat down to 170°C/340°F/gas mark 3½, toss the quinces in the juices and put the tin back in the oven for another 35–40 minutes. The compote is ready when it is a deep pinky-red and the sugar syrup is thick.

Remove the cores from the quince pieces when they have cooled and before you serve the compote.

≡ TIP ≡

Small pieces of the cooked quince can also be added to crisps and crumbles (see pages 71 and 59), or thinly sliced on a tart.

# MONT BLANC

SERVES: 6

PREP TIME: 10 MINS · COOK TIME: 2½ HOURS

WF · GF · V

3 **free-range egg whites**
¼ teaspoon **salt**
1 teaspoon **vanilla extract**
200g **caster sugar**

**FILLING:**
1 x 435g tin **sweetened chestnut purée**
300ml **double cream**, lightly whipped

*Chestnuts are the unsung heroes of the winter table. Their subtle but rich flavour is enhanced when sweetened and combined with vanilla. This is one of the classic puddings – loved by the Italians and the French, named after their favourite mountain.*

Preheat the oven to 120°C/250°F/gas mark ½. Line 2 baking trays with baking paper.

Using an electric hand mixer, beat the egg whites, salt and vanilla on a high speed until soft peaks form.

Add half the sugar to the frothy egg whites. Whisk until very stiff, then add the remaining sugar. Whisk until smooth and glossy.

Portion out 6 large meringue discs about 4cm apart on the prepared baking trays. Bake in the oven for about 2½ hours. Allow to cool on the baking trays before peeling from the paper.

When ready to serve, spoon the chestnut purée over the meringues and top with lightly whipped cream.

## ═ TIP ═

Sweetened chestnut purée, made from candied chestnuts, is available in lots of supermarkets. If you can't find it, however, you have several options:
• Buy crystallized chestnuts (marrons glacés) and purée them with a little vanilla extract, but no sugar.
• Make the purée from scratch. Buy fresh chestnuts, make a cut in each shell and boil them in water for about 10 minutes. Peel off the shells and skins and blitz the chestnuts in a food processor. Add just enough double cream to form a paste. Then add icing sugar and vanilla extract to taste.

# ROASTED PEACHES

**SERVES: 4**

**PREP TIME: 5 MINS · COOK TIME: 15 MINS**

**WF · GF · V** (**DF · Ve** if double cream is omitted)

4 ripe **white** or **yellow peaches**

8 tablespoons **white wine**

100g **caster sugar**

**double cream**, to serve (optional)

*Sometimes the best things are the simplest. Make sure you get the best peaches you can afford.*

Heat the oven to 220°C/425°F/gas mark 7.

Halve the peaches and remove the stones. Arrange the peach halves in a roasting tin, cut side up. Add the white wine and sprinkle over the caster sugar.

Bake in the oven for 12–15 minutes, until the fruit is a little golden on the edges and the syrup is bubbling. Serve with cream, if you like.

## ⇒ TIP ⇒

Use ripe delicious peaches. If they are underripe, no amount of cooking will be able to save them.

# BAKING BASICS

# FLOUR

The role of flour is to provide structure. The proteins in traditional flours react with water, producing gluten, the strands of which create a lattice in which air bubbles can be trapped, giving your baked goods 'lightness'. However, some people find gluten hard to digest. Recipes using gluten-free flours will be more cake-like, although this effect can often be offset to some degree by adding other structure providers such as eggs or gums.

## TRADITIONAL WHEAT FLOUR
*Wholemeal or white; plain, self-raising or strong (hard)*

**What is it?** Ground wheat. Wholemeal is made from the whole grain: the endosperm (proteinous/starchy), the germ (proteinous and full of vitamins), and the bran (fibrous). The other varieties of wheat flour are made from the starchy endosperm only. Plain flour is used for general baking as it produces less gluten than strong flour which is traditionally used to make bread. Self-raising flour is plain flour with a raising agent (traditionally baking powder) added.

**What is it good for?** Almost anything in traditional baking.

**Is it good for me?** For a lot of people, no. Wheat has changed beyond recognition in the past 100 years, as farmers have selectively bred it from its naturally occurring forms to the extremely high-yielding grains that are produced today. These advances have done a lot to help feed a growing global population, but at a cost.

Incidences of coeliac disease – a severe allergy to gluten, which causes the immune system to attack the lining of the small intestine – have been doubling every 15 years since the Seventies. Some people are also allergic to wheat (rather than just to the gluten it contains). In addition, wheat intolerance is a growing problem – a less catastrophic but still unpleasant reaction to modern wheat proteins which can leave you feeling heavy, tired and listless. If you are lucky enough to have a body that can cope with it, wheat is a wonderful thing. If not, there are alternatives.

## SPELT FLOUR
*Wholemeal or white*

**What is it?** Spelt is an ancient variety of wheat that has not been transformed by selective breeding.

**What is it good for?** You can use spelt as a substitute for wheat in many dishes. Although it is higher in protein than many wheat flours, it is lower in gluten. It will not therefore give you the extravagantly risen bakes that you can create with wheat flour, however it has a delicious nutty flavour. We love spelt.

**Is it good for you?** People with wheat allergy and intolerance can generally tuck into spelt quite happily. Coeliacs must avoid spelt because it contains gluten. Our own experience is that it doesn't give you that bloated sensation you get from traditional wheat.

## RYE FLOUR
**What is it?** Rye comes from the same family of grasses as wheat. It originated in Eastern Europe, where it grows well in cold climates and in poor soils. It is dense and dark and contains little gluten.

**What is it good for?** For making traditional rye breads (see page 14). Also strongly flavoured beers, vodka and whisky.

**Is it good for you?** Many people find it more palatable than wheat, as it has lower gluten levels and has been less intensively bred. It is high in vitamins and soluble fibre, and has a lower glycemic load than many wheat and spelt breads so is less likely to lead to weight gain.

## BUCKWHEAT FLOUR

**What is it?** Buckwheat is actually not a wheat at all. It is not even a grass. It is a fruit seed from the rhubarb family and similar to a sunflower seed. It is gluten free.

**What is it good for?** We use the flour to make pancakes, the flakes to make granola and porridge, and it can be used as a couscous substitute in its groat form. However, it will not provide sufficient structure to make breads unless you add eggs or xanthan gum. It can be used alongside other flours for interesting flavour and texture combinations.

**Is it good for you?** Yes. It is high in nutrients, especially manganese and magnesium, and also provides vitamins, zinc and a whole host of other goodies. It is sometimes called the 'king of the healing grains'.

## GLUTEN-FREE FLOUR

**What is it?** Any flour that does not contain gluten. You can mix your own or choose shop-bought varieties, which will generally be various blends of rice, potato, buckwheat, and bean and pea flours. They will often have added gluten substitutes such as xantham gum.

**What is it good for?** If you want to avoid gluten, you can use it as a flour substitute in instances where the dish you are making does not need the strong structure that gluten provides. In this book, we use it in crumbles, scones, cakes, tarts and bread.

**Is it good for you?** These flours will not contain gluten, but some are quite refined so they will not necessarily be packed full of nutrients.

## POLENTA

**What is it?** Coarsely ground dried corn/maize, also known as cornmeal (opposed to cornflour, which is very finely ground into a starchy white powder).

**What is it good for?** We use it to give body to cakes while avoiding wheat flour. It has a beautiful yellow colour and a mild, sweet flavour.

**Is it good for you?** It is a relatively complex carbohydrate which also contains protein and some vitamins. It's a reasonable food – it won't make a superhero of you overnight, but it isn't bad for you either.

## GRAM FLOUR

**What is it?** Ground-up dried chickpeas.

**What is it good for?** We use it to add body to some gluten-free cakes. Also good for thickening stews. It can be a little bitter, so we like to use it sparingly.

**Is it good for you?** Yes. Gluten free, it has a low glycemic load, so it won't set your sugar levels racing. Contains a good bit of protein and iron.

# LEAVENERS & THICKENERS

## 1. YEAST

A micro-organism which converts the sugars in flour into carbon dioxide bubbles, thus putting air into the dough. It comes in many forms – fresh, dried and quick-rise. We specify the type used in each recipe, but if you are substituting one for another, make sure you follow the instructions on the packet.

## 2. BICARBONATE OF SODA

A chemical compound with a slightly alkaline taste, which reacts with acids to form carbon dioxide bubbles.

## 3. BAKING POWDER

A mixture of bicarbonate of soda and an acid compound (typically cream of tartar) which reacts when moistened to produce carbon dioxide bubbles. Some baking powders use wheat as a 'moisture absorption agent'. You can buy gluten-free ones that do not.

## 4. ARROWROOT, CORNFLOUR

Starchy powders, which are useful for gluten-free binding and thickening.

## 5. XANTHUM GUM

A thickener/binder which can be used at very low concentrations to thicken sauces. Often used to help give gluten-free breads and cakes structure.

## 6. EGG SUBSTITUTE

Also known as 'whole egg replacer', it is used to replace eggs in sponges and cakes for vegans and people who are allergic. Normally made of soy protein and potato starch. Not something we use often, but nice if you are baking for a vegan.

1.

2.

4.

6.

5.

# FATS

*Fats play many roles in baking. They add moistness and tenderness. They create barriers between layers of flour, allowing crispy pastries to develop. They help gluten stretch in bread, and stop things sticking to trays.*

## 1. UNSALTED BUTTER

**What is it?** A golden block of dairy goodness made from churning cream to concentrate the butterfat. It is an emulsion of butterfat (about 80%), water and milk proteins. Unsalted butter is normally used in baking, as it has a sweeter flavour.

**What is it good for?** The most common baking fat, butter is solid at room temperature and can therefore be used to make all sorts of flaky pastries. It melts at body temperature, so it doesn't taste greasy.

**Is it good for me?** As with suet (see opposite), butter is mostly saturated fat and is therefore high in calories. These foods used to be considered the devil's work, but they are all natural and recent nutritional research suggests that (within reason) they are likely to do us less harm than processed alternatives. As it is a saturated fat, butter can also be heated without changing its structure and becoming more harmful. Butter contains very little lactose and is therefore rarely a problem for the lactose intolerant.

## 2. SALTED BUTTER

**What is it?** Butter that has had salt added as a preservative and to change the flavour.

**What is it good for?** Generally we prefer the sweeter flavour of unsalted butter in baking and puddings. Very occasionally the stronger flavour of salted butter gets the nod.

**Is it good for me?** Much the same as unsalted butter. If you need to watch your salt levels then go for unsalted.

## 3. COCONUT OIL

**What is it?** The oil extracted from coconut flesh.

**What is it good for?** It is liquid at body temperature, but just about solid at room temperature. This makes it a possible substitute for butter in many applications (although, as you will see from the recipes, you must handle it differently). Its melting point (about 23°C) is much closer to room temperature than butter (about 32°C) or indeed cocoa butter (about 34°C) – which gives it unique qualities. Coconut oil icing, for example, melts in the mouth very differently from the richer butter icings. (If you have ever tried Lindt Lindor chocolates – which contain a lot of coconut oil – you will recognize the sensation.)

**Is it good for me?** There is a great deal of debate over this. When people started cutting dairy out of their diet, coconut oil was seen as a perfect substitute. However, nutritionists pointed out that it was also high in calories and saturated fats. More recent evidence has shown that coconut oil promotes good cholesterol and that it is easily metabolized into fuel (rather than deposited as fat). Of course this is only useful if you need the fuel. Our feeling is that it is a good fat; some people say it will make you podgy, but many nutritionists disagree. Read labels carefully though, as some coconut oil is still hydrogenated. Always choose organic and unrefined.

## 4. OLIVE OIL

**What is it?** The oil extracted from olive flesh.

**What is it good for?** It is liquid at room temperature and therefore less versatile in baking than other fats discussed here. We use it in breads and pizza doughs and to toast granola.

**Is it good for you?** Yes. It is high in monounsaturated fats that may help protect against heart disease. It also contains a useful source of omega-6 fats, which we must eat because our bodies cannot make them from other foods. (Make sure you get the coldpressed variety.)

## 5. SUET

**What is it?** Raw beef (and sometimes mutton) fat, often taken from around the kidneys. The stuff that you buy in supermarkets has been dehydrated, purified and mixed with flour to stabilize it. If you use real fresh suet, you may need slightly less. (You can also buy vegetarian suet, but choose carefully: most of it is made from hydrogenated trans-fats.)

**What is it good for?** Making traditional steamed English puddings. The suet is hard and therefore forms hard pockets in the pastry. When the pudding is cooking these melt away, leaving air pockets and a wonderful light, spongy texture.

**Is it good for me?** It is a high-calorie saturated fat. However, the link between saturated fat and heart disease is now under dispute, with recent studies pointing to manufactured trans-fats and sugary foods as the real villains. Therefore: don't eat suet every day, but it's fine as an occasional treat.

## 6. LARD

**What is it?** Pig fat – often rendered (melted slowly), purified and then reset.

**What is it good for?** Generally used to make really flaky pastries (for example, the hot water crust pastry used for the pork pie on page 42). It is solid at body temperature and has a distinct soft porky flavour. We don't use it much.

**Is it good for you?** Very calorific, but probably not as sinful as its reputation would suggest. Eat it about as often as you would suet (see left).

## 7. MARGARINE

**What is it?** A butter substitute originally manufactured from beef fat but now more commonly made by thickening vegetable oils and dying them yellow.

**What is it good for?** Absolutely nothing. We don't think that any recipe tastes better when made with margarine.

**Is it good for you?** Traditional margarines, made from hydrogenating vegetable oil, were marketed as a healthier, cheaper alternative to butter. We now know that the manufacturing process created deadly trans-fats, and these types of marg have disappeared from the supermarket shelves. More recent manufacturing methods have produced a slew of products with their own advertised 'health benefits'. However, they have only recently entered the food chain and we would advise caution. Our general rule of thumb is: avoid cooking with any ingredient that was invented in the last 1,000 years.

1.

3.

5.

4.

7.

6.

2.

**12.** **7.** **8.** **1.** **5.** **10.**

It is one of the tragedies of the human condition that sweet foods were not that commonplace when our palates were evolving. To early man, sugar was a rare and valuable source of energy. As a result, we have evolved to seek it out and wolf it down. Our tastebuds, which usually guide us towards things that are good for us, tell us that sweet things are to be gobbled up with abandon.

Until as recently as 1766, when the Sugar Tax was repealed, it was impossible to get hold of sugar in sufficient quantity to do us harm. But white processed sugar is now cheap and plentiful, and over the last couple of decades has been recognized (alongside processed carbohydrates) as the single greatest threat to our health. In the end, moderation is the answer, but there are some sweet substances out there that enable us to satisfy those evolutionary instincts while offering a little more protection to our bodies.

**6.** **9.** **11.** **3.** **4.**

**2.**

# SUGAR

Sugar is made by distilling a sweet syrup – usually taken from sugar cane or sugar beet – until it crystallizes. It is almost irresistible. We try to use substitutes where possible. Where you do use it, here are a few rules:

**Use cane sugar** (preferably Fairtrade), not beet sugar. Beet sugar has a funny taste, particularly noticeable in icings.
**Use unrefined sugar** – it has a slightly nicer taste and at least retains some minerals and nutrients.
**Eat as a treat only.** Otherwise it will make your blood sugar soar and then slump, leaving you moody and, later, a bit fatter.

Sugar comes in many forms from white caster sugar to dark brown muscovado. If you are ever holidaying in a sugar-producing country, take an afternoon off the beach to visit a sugar refinery. They are amazing places. The cane is ground by vast grooved metal rollers sprayed with hot water, and the resulting syrup is boiled to varying levels of darkness in bubbling vats. The smell is intoxicating. Unrefined sugars are spun off from the syrups at varying levels of concentration (each darker than the last), using a centrifuge. The final remaining sweet syrup is called molasses, which is dense in nutrients compared to other sugars. Some sugars used frequently in baking are:

## 1. UNREFINED CASTER SUGAR

Unrefined means it contains molasses; refined sugar has this source of nutrients and flavour removed. Unrefined cane sugar comes from an early stage of distillation, and the brown of the molasses is hardly visible. The crystals are ground, which makes them easy to mix, melt and dissolve.

## 2. UNREFINED DEMERARA SUGAR

Darker than caster sugar, with a stronger flavour. Larger crystals give it a satisfyingly crunchy bite.

## 3. DARK BROWN MUSCOVADO SUGAR

This sugar is not spun in the centrifuge, but is left to dry in the sun. It therefore contains more plant matter, which gives it its rich flavour. It is very different from, and much nicer than, the brown sugar made by adding molasses to white sugar.

## 4. ICING SUGAR

A very finely ground refined sugar, which generally contains an anti-caking agent.

## 5. TREACLE

The syrup left over when the sugar crystals have been spun out. Light treacle (or golden syrup) is made from the by-product of the first white sugar production. Black treacle is made from later boilings and contains more plant matter and less sugar (about 55% sugar). It is similar to molasses.

## 6. FRUCTOSE

The sugar in cane sugar is sucrose, which is made up of glucose and fructose (the latter also occurs naturally in fruit). Sugar can be treated to create fructose, which is less likely to give you a sugar high followed by a sugar low. However, there is recent evidence to suggest that it might turn to fat more easily than other sugars. In this book we therefore use a number of other natural sweeteners.

# NATURAL SWEETENERS

Natural sweeteners are generally used because they cause less of a sugar rush than traditional sugar and are less refined, containing more nutrients. They still come with some caveats.

## 7. HONEY

Flower nectar collected by bees.

**What is good about it?** Natural and delicious. Many forms are high in fructose and therefore create less of a sugar rush.

**Any problems?** Much mass-market honey is made by feeding the bees sugar syrup – and so is nutritionally identical to sugar.

## 8. MAPLE SYRUP

A syrup from the sap of maple trees.

**What is good about it?** Like honey, it is natural and delicious.
**Any problems?** The sweetness comes mostly from sucrose, and therefore it carries the same health warnings as sugar.

## 9. AGAVE NECTAR

A syrup produced from the Mexican agave plant. It is sweeter than honey, but less viscous.

**What is good about it?** It tastes good and is much less likely to give you a sugar rush.

**Any problems?** Due to massive recent demand, much of it is now quite heavily processed.

## 10. BROWN RICE SYRUP

This is derived by culturing cooked rice with enzymes from dried barley sprouts to break down the starches, which is then strained off and the resulting sweet liquid cooked.

**What is good about it?** It is a natural product that will not give you a sugar rush and does not contain fructose.

**Any problems?** It is strongly flavoured. It has not been widely available for long, but so far seems to be fairly harmless.

## 11. YACON SYRUP

A dark molasses-like syrup made from a Peruvian root.

**What is good about it?** Unlike agave syrup, the compounds providing the sweetness in yacon syrup pass through the body without being metabolized at all.

**Any problems?** It has a pretty strong flavour. As yet, no one has claimed that it is bad for you.

## 12. STEVIA

A mint-like herb that is very sweet but contains no calories. Has been hailed as the potential solution to the sugar problem.

**What is good about it?** Sweet without an aftertaste and contains no calories. Will not give you a sugar rush.

**Any problems?** It used to be almost impossible to get hold of, but there is an increasing number of products now available.

# BAKING WITH ALTERNATIVES

Baking with alternatives to wheat flour, butter and white sugar is easier than you might think. Think of these alternatives not as replacement ingredients but as new ones to experiment with. If you don't go in much for experimentation in the kitchen, don't worry, we have done most of the work for you already. All tried and tested, and this is one situation where curiosity definitely won't kill the cat.

To be more experimental, try using these ingredients in your own recipes. You may need a bit of good old-fashioned trial and error before they work out, but to help you, here are some rules which will let you predict how they may behave.

## Flours
Rice flour is a great alternative to wheat if used in conjunction with a little xanthan gum, which is a good stand-in for gluten. Without it, cakes can crumble a bit too much. Rice flour has a slightly coarser texture than that of wheat flour. The finely ground rice has a crumbly texture which is similar to ground almonds and different from the light texture of wheat flour. It lies somewhere between wheat and maize flour.

Though corn and oats are alright for some people, they are not suitable for everyone with a wheat and gluten intolerance. We have tried to include recipes for everyone. Ready-mixed gluten-free flours are an easy way to take your favourite recipe and make it suitable for you.

## Sweeteners
Wherever caster sugar is called for, this is usually not just for sweetness but also for its structural qualities. For that reason, be cautious about using substitutes. You could, however, use a slightly less refined sugar such as golden caster sugar.

Agave nectar is a wonderful sweetener and much easier for our bodies to digest than sugar. It is also suitable for those who can't have sugar or honey. It takes longer to absorb into the bloodstream as well, so your blood sugar doesn't go haywire. We also love maple syrup, but it is very expensive.

## Dairy & egg alternatives
Coconut oil is a very exciting discovery if you are staying away from dairy. It makes fantastic icing (though you'll need to chill it a bit, as it stays liquid at a lower temperature than butter). It also works very well baked in some cakes.

If soya milk agrees with you, you'll find it great to bake with. Rice milk and coconut milk are very good too, but a little different in texture. We use cashew nut butter in our vanilla icing, along with soy (or rice) milk and coconut oil, and the creamy texture is a dream.

Egg alternatives are easier to find than you might expect. A little ground flax meal or chia seed makes a great nutritional substitute. You can also use apple sauce to get the right texture in cakes. Commercial egg replacers are usually just soy and potato starch, which are thickeners.

# TECHNIQUES

- - - - - - - - - - - - - - - - - - - - - - - - - - - - - - - - - - - - - - - - - - - - -

*Although all the recipes in this book contain enough instructions for you to plunge straight in, what follows is intended as a sort of mini masterclass in baking techniques.*

- - - - - - - - - - - - - - - - - - - - - - - - - - - - - - - - - - - - - - - - - - - - -

## 1. GENERAL TIPS

### Make notes

You never know when you will try an experiment that creates something wonderful. Get into the habit of having a pencil and paper to hand to jot down what you have done.

### If you are substituting ingredients, be prepared to experiment a little

For example, if you use spelt flour in place of wholemeal flour, or fructose instead of sugar, you will find that their properties are different. They will produce different textures, absorb different amounts of liquid, and so on. Don't let this put you off experimentation – just be aware of it and observe the results in case you want to tweak the recipes next time.

### Measure everything out first

Chefs call this *mise en place* – literally, 'put in place'. It makes the whole process more ordered and enjoyable. If you are a man, there is a chance that you will forget this advice.

## 2. MIXING AND MEASURING

### Weigh water on your scales

As mentioned previously, measuring jugs can give you a close reading of volume but weighing water leaves less margin for error. Water is the same in weight by grams as its volume in millilitres (1g = 1ml). Milk works like this, too. But some liquids

(such as honey) are denser and so weigh a little more than their volume, or are less dense (like cream), so weigh less. For this reason you're better off measuring these.

### Sifting

Put the ingredients that you want to sift into a large sieve held over a bowl. Tip the sieve to an angle of 30° and knock the lower edge repeatedly with a metal spoon or the back of a knife until everything has passed through. With icing sugar, you might have to crush the last few balls through with the back of a spoon.

### Combining dry ingredients

Sometimes sifting is not necessary. If you don't mind lumps, and are only trying to evenly distribute raising agents or spices through a large quantity of flour, using a hand-held whisk is a great shortcut.

### Creaming

There are two ways to cream your butter and sugar. The recipes in this book will each say which one to use.

*The traditional method* – this method is slightly more painstaking, but gives the lightest cakes. You mix the butter (softened) vigorously with the sugar (ideally with an electric mixer) to trap air. You then mix in the other ingredients gradually in the following order – eggs, then some flour, then some liquid, then the rest of the flour, then the rest of the liquid.

*The two-stage mixing method* – more common in America – produces soft but slightly heavier cakes. It is quicker. You mix all the dry ingredients in one bowl, then mix the butter into those (as if making pastry) before adding the wet ingredients until incorporated.

### Folding

This is how you mix two semi-liquid substances while preserving the air trapped in one of them (for example melted chocolate and whisked egg, or fruit purée and whipped cream). We were taught slightly different ways to fold, but the principle remains the same – do it gently and without any obviously 'crushing' or 'deflating' motions.

*Claire's method:* Use a rubber spatula to gently but quickly fold together aerated eggs or cream with other ingredients. Swirls will form in the mixture but don't worry about mixing until they are gone, as you run the risk of overmixing.

*Henry's method:* Put the mixture with the air in it on top of the other mixture in a large bowl. Take a large metal spoon and cut vertically down into the middle of the bowl. When you hit the bottom, scoop the spoon around towards you, gently lifting the mixture and folding it back on top of the bowl. Rotate the bowl by 45° and repeat until mixed.

## 3. PASTRY – THE BASICS

### General tips

When making most pastries the trick is to trap little pieces of butter within a dough, which melt when you cook it and create something flaky and delicious as the water from the butter evaporates and turns to steam, which rises, pushing up the layers. Unless otherwise stated, therefore, make sure that all your ingredients are cold and that you make it in a cold room (if the butter melts before you cook it you will get something dense rather than light and flaky).

Always rest a dough in the fridge for at least half an hour before rolling it out. This allows the gluten to relax, which will make the task much easier.

When rolling out pastry for a tart tin, lift the pressure as you get to the edge of the dough to avoid making it too thin.

Your pastry will vary depending on the type of flour you use, the fats, the humidity, the temperature and so on. If you are keen to perfect the art, observe closely what happens each time you make a certain type of pastry and take notes. Over time you will learn when an extra splash of water or a sift of flour are required.

### Basic pastries

The basic kinds of pastries that we use in this book are flaky, shortcrust and pressed-crust. Flaky pastry has thin layers of fat separating thin layers of dough and will break into thin flakes. Shortcrust and pressed-crust pastries crumble into small pieces, as the fat has been worked through the flour. We provide recipes for these with the main recipes as appropriate, but thought it would be useful to give the basics here for easy reference – see overleaf.

Henry thinks life is a bit too short to be making your own puff pastry – you can now buy some very good all-butter versions from the supermarket.

# SHORTCRUST PASTRY

**MAKES: 300G**

200g **plain flour**

a pinch of **salt**

75g **unsalted butter**, cut into rough
1cm cubes

2½ tablespoons cold **water**

Sift the flour and salt and add the butter. Rub the mixture gently between your fingertips until it resembles coarse sand.

Sprinkle the water over the mixture and mix until it forms a cohesive ball of dough.

Wrap the pastry in clingfilm and allow to rest in the fridge for at least 30 minutes before using.

# PRESSED-CRUST PASTRY

**MAKES ENOUGH FOR A 20–23CM FLAN TIN**

140g **plain flour**

2 tablespoons **caster sugar**

100g **unsalted butter**, melted

1 tablespoon **white vinegar**

Blend the ingredients briefly in a food processor and pat into a tart tin.

# FLAKY PASTRY

The same ingredients as the shortcrust pastry above but keep the pieces of butter larger and don't mix them in all the way.

## 4. EGGS

**Buying eggs**

Choose a decent-sized, free-range egg. Chickens that have been well fed and cared for produce yolks that are more yellow and lustrous. The yellow or orange yolks are also indicative of the seasons, as the greener the grass that the chickens are eating, the deeper the colour of the yolks.

**Storing eggs**

If you live in a cold climate or are using your eggs within a matter of days, you can keep them out of the fridge. If you are planning to keep them for a while, or there is a heatwave, put them into the fridge (preferably in an airtight box to keep out smells from other foods, which can permeate the shells).

**Bringing eggs to temperature**

When baking, eggs should be at room temperature. If you are getting them from the fridge, you can plunge them into warm water for a couple of minutes to speed up the process.

**Breaking eggs**

Break the shells against a flat worktop, rather than against the edge of the bowl or with a knife or spoon. This way, pieces of shell are less likely to get forced into the egg.

**Separating eggs**

Holding the two halves of the broken egg above a bowl, plop the yolk from one half shell to the other, back and forth, until all the white has fallen into the bowl. Then drop the yolk into another, smaller bowl. (If the yolk starts to break up, move fast and get the yolk into the yolks bowl. It is better to have a little white in the yolks bowl than a little yolk in the whites bowl. Yolk contamination makes it harder, if not impossible, to whisk the whites to soft peaks, see below.)

**Whisking egg whites**

This is one of the few cases where fresher is not better. It is actually slightly easier to whisk the whites of older, runnier eggs. MAKE SURE THE BOWL AND THE WHISK ARE VERY CLEAN. A little dirt – particularly fat, which you find in egg yolks – can prevent a good voluminous cloud of whites. A pinch of salt or cream of tartar helps the whisking. Be careful not to over-whisk egg whites: once they have formed stiff peaks, whisking them further will cause them to break down.

# QUICK CUSTARD

MAKES: 600ML
PREP TIME: 5 MINS · COOK TIME: 15 MINS
WF · GF · V

1 **vanilla pod**, split lengthwise

500ml **double cream**

100ml **milk**

180g **caster sugar**

5 **free-range egg yolks**, at room
temperature

a pinch of **sea salt**

*By using more cream than in most recipes, and – critically – heating the sugar with the cream, rather than adding it to the egg yolks, this recipe avoids the nervous stage of heating the custard over the stove and waiting for it to thicken – or, more often than not, scramble.*

Put the vanilla pod into a pan with the cream, milk and caster sugar. Bring to the boil, stirring to make sure the sugar dissolves. Take the pan off the heat and allow it to sit for 5 minutes.

Meanwhile, put your egg yolks into a blender and blend for 2 minutes, or until they go creamy. Add a small pinch of salt.

Bring the cream back to the boil, remove the vanilla pod, and pour the mixture slowly into the eggs, blending as you go. Assuming that the cream was good and hot and the eggs not too cold, you should be left with great not-too-thick custard. (If you want to make it thicker, heat it gently on the hob, but you shouldn't need to.)

## 5. MAKING CAKES

Here are some tips to help you avoid common errors when making cakes.

### Creaming butter & eggs to avoid curdling

To help avoid curdling, always bring your ingredients to room temperature before you start. Your butter should be very, very soft. Whip the butter and sugar together with an electric hand whisk. It is so much easier than doing it by hand, and you will get enough air into the mixture to be able to hold the eggs. The butter and sugar mixture is ready when it has doubled in volume and turned almost white.

Add the eggs one by one, fully incorporating each addition.

If you're making a cake that has lots of eggs (such as a Victoria sponge), add a teaspoon or two of flour to help stabilize the mixture, but not too much or the cake may become tough.

### Slow & low

If in doubt when making a cake, bake it slow and low for greater moistness throughout. The name of this method came from a rap song that Claire is particularly fond of. 'Slow and low that is the tempo' is the lyric, and it has become her baking mantra.

### Avoiding domed cakes

There are two main reasons why cakes sometimes dome up in the middle.

(a) The metal on the outside of the pan conducts the heat faster. The sides of the cake set while the centre still continues to bake and rise.

(b) The structure of the cake is too strong, preventing the leavening gases from escaping until towards the end of baking, when they erupt through the centre in little tunnels. The mixture may have been mixed too much after the flour was added, and the air bubbles try to escape through the middle. When glutens form, the crumb becomes dry and tough.

### Avoiding sunken cakes

If a cake has bicarbonate of soda in it and no acid (such as cream of tartar) to neutralize it, it can rise at first and then fall down. (Note: if a recipe calls for baking powder and you do not have any available, a mix of bicarbonate of soda and cream of tartar can be substituted.)

Always check the expiration dates on your leavening powders. They don't last forever, and expired leavening powders are the source of many failed cakes.

Too much mixture in the cake tin can cause a cake to sink in the middle. When baking a sponge, always leave about a quarter of the tin unfilled to give the cake room to rise up. Fruit cakes won't rise as much, so you can fill the tin a bit more. Sinking can also be a sign that your cake is under-baked.

Try not to rush the cooling of a cake. As cake cools, it continues to bake very slightly. Rushing it might mean it sinks.

### To test for doneness

There are three ways to test for doneness.

The skewer method: Good for denser cakes. Insert a skewer (or a long thin knife) into the centre of the cake, and when it pulls out clean, the cake is done.

The listening method: Henry's mother-in-law, Petra (see page 114), swears by this for fruit cakes. Open the oven door, take out the cake and listen. A fruit cake will 'hiss' gently while it cooks, or as Petra says 'sings'. When it stops 'singing', it is done.

The pressing method: Good for lighter cakes such as sponges. Press down gently on the top of the cake: when it springs back, rather than leaving a slight dent, it is done.

Be sure to use the right method, as not every method works for every cake. Some cakes are meant to be moist, so the skewer test isn't foolproof. The spring-back-to-the-touch test is not sufficient if a cake is supposed to be soft. The 'listening' method works best for fruit cakes, and the timer is never to be trusted.

## Fan-assisted ovens

Often cookbooks will ask you to put the cake in the middle of the oven, because heat rises and the top can be hotter than the bottom. Modern fan-assisted ovens are very efficient at circulating heat evenly around the oven, so there's no need to worry about positioning.

Even if you have a few racks filled, the heat will be pushed by the fan all around the baking cakes.

All the recipes in this book have been tested without a fan, with the cakes positioned on the middle shelf of the oven. If you are using a fan-assisted oven, lower the given temperature by 20°C.

# 6. DOUGH

## Kneading

When kneading dough by hand, remember that you are trying to stretch the gluten. This requires energy. Henry likes to break a sweat when making and baking bread.

He says if you are not breaking a sweat, you are not working it hard enough. Big long stretches with the ball of the hand are the thing. Claire is a fan of the slap and tickle method: stretching the dough up and out, then slapping it down on to a work surface rather than using the pushing method.

The idea with this method is to incorporate air into the dough whilst kneading and to form the gluten so that you don't need to add as much flour to the bread. Both methods will produce equally beautiful bread.

# 7. ICING

There are three main icings that we use in this book – basic, buttercream and royal.

**Basic** is a mixture of water (or fruit juice or purée) and icing sugar, and forms a delicate, flat crispy coating when set.

**Royal icing** is similar to basic icing, but uses egg white to make it harden to a much more brittle texture (think about Christmas cake icing).

**Buttercream icing** is a rich and creamy mixture of sugar, butter and flavourings. Claire has also come up with a vegan version of buttercream icing using coconut oil, soya and agave nectar.

You can find recipes for icings on the following pages:

# 8. STORING

### Cakes, bread & biscuits
These should all be wrapped in greaseproof paper and kept in an airtight container at room temperature. Storing them in the fridge will make them go stale more quickly (starches crystallize faster at colder temperatures). Bread freezes well. Try slicing it and storing it in airtight bags, then toasting it straight from the freezer.

### Baking ingredients
Any ingredients that live in the fridge are best kept in an airtight container to stop them picking up smells from other foods. It's also best to keep flour, sugar and other larder ingredients in airtight containers to keep the damp out.

### Sterilizing jars
To sterilize, put clean, washed and dried jam jars or bottles into a cold oven with the lids off. Turn the oven on to 170°C/340°F/gas mark 3½ and put the timer on for 20 minutes. When the bell goes, turn off the oven, leaving the jars inside. Pour in your jam, jelly, chutney or syrup while the jars are still hot.

# 9. SUBSTITUTES

### Baking powder & plain flour v. self-raising
If you only have plain flour on hand and a recipe calls for self-raising, you can add a teaspoon of baking powder for every 140g of plain flour.

### Substitutes for buttermilk
Buttermilk and yoghurt make cakes soft and moist because of their acidity. Buttermilk is becoming more readily available in the UK, probably because of the fashion for American-style baking.

If you don't have buttermilk, you can use half plain yoghurt and half whole milk. Another alternative is to use 1 tablespoon of fresh lemon juice with 200ml milk – this will make the equivalent of 225ml of buttermilk.

### Substitutes for brown sugar
If you have no brown sugar, add 1 tablespoon of molasses or black treacle to 200g of caster or granulated sugar to get the right flavour.

# INDEX

# ABOUT THE AUTHORS

**CLAIRE PTAK** is former Pastry Chef at the legendary California restaurant Chez Panisse, and now chef-proprietor of Violet Cakes in London. She was chosen to make Prince Harry and Meghan Markle's wedding cake. Claire hosts Violet Sessions, a podcast that explores culture, creativity, work and lifestyle through conversations with fascinating women. She is author of *The Violet Bakery Cookbook*, *The Home-Made Sweet Shop*, *Sweets, Candy & Chocolates*, *The Whoopie Pie Book* and *LEON Baking & Puddings*.

**HENRY DIMBLEBY** was co-founder of healthy fast food chain, LEON. With John Vincent and Allegra McEvedy, the first branch was opened in London in July 2004, and six months after opening, LEON was named the Best New Restaurant in Great Britain at the *Observer Food Monthly* Awards.

**LEON** now has more than 60 restaurants (including branches in Washington, DC, Amsterdam, Utrecht and Oslo). The first LEON cookbook was published in 2008 and a decade on, the range now includes 15 titles.

*To George, Johnny, and Dory for their unshakeable conviction that I am the best cook in the world. And to my wife, Mima, who makes everyone around her feel they have so much to give. – HD*

*For Damian and Shuggie. – CP*

An Hachette UK Company
www.hachette.co.uk

First published in Great Britain in 2019 by
Conran Octopus Limited, an imprint of
Octopus Publishing Group Ltd
Carmelite House
50 Victoria Embankment
London EC4Y 0DZ
www.octopusbooks.co.uk

Except for the recipes on pages 128–129, 142–143, 160–161 and 164–165, the recipes in this book were previously published in *Leon Baking & Puddings*.

ISBN 978 1 84091 792 5

A CIP catalogue record for this book is available from the British Library.

Printed and bound in China

10 9 8 7 6 5 4 3 2 1

Publisher: Alison Starling
Assistant Editor: Emily Brickell
Creative Director: Jonathan Christie
Design: Ella McLean
Senior Production Manager: Katherine Hockley

Special Photography: Steven Joyce
(Photography on pages 204 and 223: Georgia Glynn Smith)
Food styling: Sian Henley
Food styling assistants: Grace Evans, Anna Hiddlestone and Libby Silbermann
Prop styling: Lauren Law

All the recipes in this book have been tested without a fan, with the cakes positioned on the middle shelf of the oven. If you are using a fan-assisted oven, lower the given temperature by 20°C.

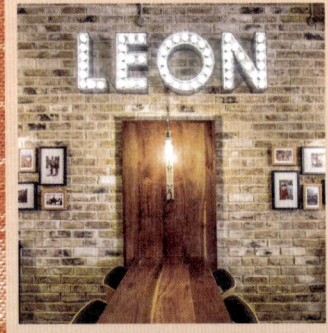